Cambridge Elements ☰

Elements in Campaigns and Elections
edited by
R. Michael Alvarez
California Institute of Technology
Emily Beaulieu Bacchus
University of Kentucky
Charles Stewart III
Massachusetts Institute of Technology

THE POWER OF POLLS?

A Cross-National Experimental Analysis of the Effects of Campaign Polls

Jason Roy
Wilfrid Laurier University

Shane P. Singh
University of Georgia

Patrick Fournier
Université de Montréal

CAMBRIDGE
UNIVERSITY PRESS

CAMBRIDGE
UNIVERSITY PRESS

University Printing House, Cambridge CB2 8BS, United Kingdom

One Liberty Plaza, 20th Floor, New York, NY 10006, USA

477 Williamstown Road, Port Melbourne, VIC 3207, Australia

314–321, 3rd Floor, Plot 3, Splendor Forum, Jasola District Centre,
New Delhi – 110025, India

103 Penang Road, #05–06/07, Visioncrest Commercial, Singapore 238467

Cambridge University Press is part of the University of Cambridge.

It furthers the University's mission by disseminating knowledge in the pursuit of
education, learning, and research at the highest international levels of excellence.

www.cambridge.org
Information on this title: www.cambridge.org/9781108792462
DOI: 10.1017/9781108877428

© Jason Roy, Shane P. Singh, and Patrick Fournier 2021

First published 2021

A catalogue record for this publication is available from the British Library.

ISBN 978-1-108-79246-2 Paperback
ISSN 2633-0970 (online)
ISSN 2633-0962 (print)

Cambridge University Press has no responsibility for the persistence or accuracy of
URLs for external or third-party internet websites referred to in this publication
and does not guarantee that any content on such websites is, or will remain,
accurate or appropriate.

The Power of Polls?

A Cross-National Experimental Analysis of the Effects of Campaign Polls

Elements in Campaigns and Elections

DOI: 10.1017/9781108877428
First published online: September 2021

Jason Roy
Wilfrid Laurier University

Shane P. Singh
University of Georgia

Patrick Fournier
Université de Montréal

Author for correspondence: Jason Roy, jroy@wlu.ca

Abstract: Public opinion polls have become increasingly prominent during elections, but how they affect voting behaviour remains uncertain. In this work, we estimate the effects of poll exposure using an experimental design in which we randomly assign the availability of polls to participants in simulated election campaigns. We draw upon results from ten independent experiments conducted across six countries on four continents (Argentina, Australia, Canada, New Zealand, the United Kingdom, and the United States) to examine how polls affect the amount of information individuals seek and the votes that they cast. We further assess how poll effects differ according to individual-level factors, such as partisanship and political sophistication, and the content included in polls and how it is presented. Our work provides a comprehensive assessment of the power of polls and the implications for poll reporting in contemporary elections.

Keywords: Political behaviour, Public opinion polls, Elections, Information search, Vote choice, Experiments

ISBNs: 9781108792462 (PB), 9781108877428 (OC)
ISSNs: 2633-0970 (online), 2633-0962 (print)

Contents

1. Do Polls Matter?

Public opinion polls are ubiquitous in politics.[1] This is especially true in the lead-up to elections, when citizens are expected to perform their primary democratic responsibility. The prominence of polls during election campaigns is extensive. For instance, the website fivethirtyeight.com counted 1,084 national polls regarding the 2016 presidential race in the United States (US) that were released in the 10 months prior to election day. In the United Kingdom (UK), Mark Pack's PollBase reports 325 national election polls conducted during 2019. The same UK data can help us visualize the dramatic increase in the availability of poll results over time. Figure 1.1 shows the quantity of national electoral polls released during the two-month period that preceded each election since World War II. During electoral campaigns in the 1980s, 1990s and 2000s, British citizens were exposed to approximately one poll per day on average. Over the last decade, that number has risen even higher, reaching a mean close to two polls per day. A similar surge in election polling is also evident in the US (e.g., Traugott 2005; Erikson and Wlezien 2012).

Opinion polls have also become an increasingly common feature of pre-election media coverage. One form of political reporting that has become more prevalent in many countries in recent decades, particularly during campaigns, is known as horserace or game-framing journalism (Broh 1980; Wilson 1981; Brady and Johnston 1987; Sigelman and Bullock 1991; Mendelsohn 1993; Patterson 1993; Brettschneider 1997; Craig 2000; Iyengar, Norpoth, and Hahn 2004; Soroka and Andrew 2010; Aalberg, Strömbäck and de Vreese 2012; Dimitrova and Kostadinova 2013; Schuck et al. 2013; Dunaway and Lawrence 2015; Schmuck et al. 2017). This style of reporting limits coverage of more substantive issues, focusing instead on how well candidates or parties are doing: who is in front, who is behind, who is gaining momentum, and who is losing ground. Public opinion polls provide much of the fodder for this style of journalism, which has been remarkably intense during electoral periods—precisely the time when voters are called upon to weigh the political options available to them and to select their representatives. In addition, the rise of data journalism has contributed to the presence of polls in media reports during elections (Coddington 2015; Splendore et al. 2016). Altogether, there is little doubt that polls have become a dominant part of contemporary election campaigns.

---

[1] With the term public opinion poll, we are referring to information (e.g., vote intentions, policy preferences, issue positions) drawn from a sample of a larger population of citizens. In what follows, our use of the term refers exclusively to a measure of public vote intentions in the lead-up to an election.

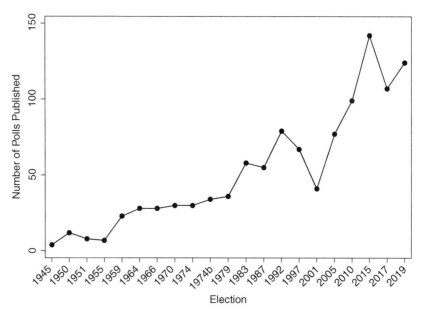

Figure 1.1: The Number of Polls Published During UK Election Campaigns, 1945–2019

Note: Data from https://www.markpack.org.uk/opinion-polls/

Given the prominence of election polls across democracies, their accuracy warrants consideration. Unlike most attitudes and behaviours estimated with surveys, it is possible to compare campaign poll results to the thing they are meant to estimate: the distribution of party or candidate support in the voting population on election day. When election outcomes differ from pre-election poll projections, these polling errors reflect a lack of accuracy (Jennings and Wlezien 2018), and they receive considerable attention. For example, a straw poll by the Literary Digest magazine famously predicted the wrong winner in the 1936 American presidential election (Alf Landon rather than Franklin Roosevelt), while newcomer poll houses headed by Crossley, Gallup and Roper that employed more rigorous sampling methods made quite accurate predictions (Gosnell 1937). However, these same polling companies encountered failure the following decade: they all erroneously expected defeats by Harry Truman at the hands of Thomas Dewey in 1948 (Mosteller et al. 1949). Other historical polling fiascos include the 1970 British general election (Abrams 1970), the 1992 British election (Jowell et al. 1993), and the 2002 French presidential election (Durand, Blais, and Larochelle 2004). More recently, polls overestimated support for the option to remain in the European Union during the 2016 Brexit referendum in the United Kingdom, and they incorrectly projected the Conservative Party's lead over the Labour Party in the 2015 and 2017 British elections (Sturgis et al. 2016; Jennings 2019). Sometimes, poll failures are more imagined than real. Case in point, during the 2016 American presidential contest, national polls predicted fairly accurately the victory of Hillary Clinton over Donald Trump in the popular vote, though polls failed to anticipate Trump's triumph in the Electoral College and in some state-level races (Kennedy et al. 2018).

In fact, comparisons between actual election results and end-of-campaign poll predictions tend to show that deviations are rather small, despite the fact they regularly fall outside the statistical margin of error (e.g., Felson and Sudman 1975; Buchanan 1986; Erikson and Sigelman 1995; Curtice 1997; Mitofsky 1998; Traugott 2001, 2005; Sanders 2003; Crewe 2005; Magalhães 2005; Panagopoulos 2009; Erikson and Wlezien 2012; Panagopoulos and Farrer 2014; Wright, Farrar, and Russell 2014; Jennings and Wlezien 2018). There are exceptions of course, and poll failures get more media coverage than poll successes.[2] But overall, evidence suggests that, most of the time, polls reflect reality quite well. Furthermore, a large study of 351 elections in 45 countries between 1942 and 2017 shows that the level of accuracy of polls has remained essentially stable across time and space (Jennings and Wlezien 2018). It is also noteworthy that polls are not becoming less reliable, despite the recent move toward less expensive, non-traditional approaches and methods, such as internet panels (Baker et al. 2010; Callegaro et al. 2014).

Whether opinion polls are accurate or not, some people fear that citizens may be unduly swayed by being exposed to the level of public support for each candidate or party. Could polling information lead some individuals to be less politically engaged, more cynical, less inclined to turnout, or more likely to change their mind about for whom they vote?

In response to these concerns, many countries enforce a ban on the dissemination of polling results for a period of time during elections. While the UK and the US do not have restrictions on the publication of polls, 40% of countries around the world impose a polling blackout according to the ACE Electoral Knowledge Network (aceproject.org). Of the 93 countries that do so, 52 limit the embargo to the last 1–3 days of the campaign and/or election day (such as Australia, Canada, and France), while 22 countries ban the release of polls for more than a week: notably Argentina

---

[2] Polling catastrophes also generate investigations that produce lessons and recommendations to improve subsequent polls. For illustrations, see the references in the previous paragraph.

(8 days), Chile (15 days), Greece (15 days), Italy (15 days), Japan (12–17 days), and Taiwan (10 days).[3]

Are such restrictions warranted? Should we be worried about the effects of polling results on people's attitudes and behaviours? Not surprisingly, these concerns have prompted much scholarly attention to the influence of polls on citizens over the last half-century.

1.1. Past Research on the Influence of Polls on Citizens

The bulk of previous work has concentrated on the effects of public opinion polls on three core political inclinations and behaviours: people's willingness to express an opinion, electoral participation, and vote choice. In this study, we consider only the latter of these three areas, vote choice. In addition, we tackle a much less common consideration: how poll exposure affects the information search. We continue this section with a brief overview of the scholarship to date on the ways in which polls influence opinion expression and turnout, followed by a more detailed discussion of how polls may impact vote choice. We then lay out our theory regarding the effects of polls on a citizen's information search and vote choice.

The first strand of polling research revolves around the spiral of silence theory proposed by Elisabeth Noëlle-Neumann (1974; 1993). This theory suggests that when individuals believe that their personal opinion on a topic—including vote intention—is congruent with majority public sentiment, they have no problem expressing that opinion publicly. However, when individuals believe that their opinion is only shared by a minority of the population, they are less likely to state it publicly because of a fear of isolation. Quite simply, people tend not to want to appear as social deviants.

Empirical work testing this theory does not necessarily rely on awareness of polling results. Generally, citizens' perceptions of dominant public opinion are used, since the theory explicitly argues that citizens can sense majority preferences in their social environment without any detailed knowledge of poll numbers. Study designs vary: correlations between the perceived opinion climate and the tendency to voice opinions in individual-level survey data (e.g., Lasorsa 1991; Matthes, Morrison, and Schemer 2010), trends over time in aggregate survey data (e.g., Katz and Baldassare 1994; Shamir 1997), individual dynamics in panel survey data (e.g., McDonald et al. 2001; Matthes 2015), and experiments where the opinion climate is manipulated (e.g., Hayes 2007; Rios and Chen 2014). Although findings sometimes are not

---

[3] See aceproject.org for a more detailed review of cross-national regulations pertaining to the dissemination of pre-election poll results.

supportive (e.g., Katz and Baldassare 1992; Huang 2005), several meta-analyses confirm the existence of a small but significant relationship between the opinion climate and individuals' propensity to express an opinion (Glynn, Hayes, and Shanahan 1997; Glynn and Huge 2014; Matthes, Knoll, and von Sikorski 2018). Minority status fosters silence, no matter on which continent the study is conducted, whether the study is observational or experimental, whether participants are students or not, whether expression occurs online or offline, or whether the climate refers to the entire population or a close reference group; but the effect is more pronounced for issues that are obtrusive and relevant to people's lives, as well as when expression targets family and friends rather than strangers (Matthes et al. 2018).

The second strand of research ascertains whether the presence of opinion polls affects the number of people who cast a ballot on election day. One argument is that polls could decrease turnout by depicting the outcome of the election as already determined, thereby discouraging people from making the effort of going to the voting station (Niemi, Iusi, and Bianco 1983). Some relevant research does not actually look at pre-election polls, but instead examines whether election night coverage, exit polls, and outcome projections in earlier time zones have an impact on turnout in later time zones where voting is still possible. If turnout in late-voting areas is dampened by an early media announcement of a victory on election day, it seems reasonable to expect that campaign polls reporting a lopsided distribution of vote intentions might have similar potential. The first studies of this type failed to find a clear relationship (Fuchs 1966; Mendelsohn 1966; Lang and Lang 1968; Mendelsohn and Crespi 1970; Tuchman and Coffin 1971; Epstein and Strom 1981). But subsequent work uncovered a notable drop in turnout in later time zones (Wolfinger and Linquiti 1981; Dubois 1983; Jackson 1983; Delli Carpini 1984; Sudman 1986; Morton et al. 2015).

Other studies deal with the link between pre-election polls and electoral turnout indirectly, by turning to the consequences of campaign media attention focusing on the horserace. Combining the 2008 Austrian National Election Study with content analysis, Lengauer and Höller (2012) document that exposure to horserace coverage has a negative effect on voter participation. Analogous conclusions are reached by an experimental study in which the nature of media frames is manipulated: focusing on the horserace supresses turnout intentions, civic duty and political trust, particularly among non-partisans and the less educated (Valentino, Beckmann, and Buhr 2001).

Of course, in line with the rational choice model of voting (e.g., Downs 1957; Riker and Ordeshook 1968), the extent to which polls increase or decrease turnout should depend upon whether or not they indicate a tight race—and thus influence whether individuals believe that their participation can be pivotal.

There is ample evidence that the closeness of election day voting results is positively associated with turnout (see notably Cox and Munger 1989; Blais 2000, 2006; Geys 2006; Cancela and Geys 2016).[4] Scholars have also hunted for signs that polling information about the closeness of the race during the campaign increases turnout. Some draw upon observational evidence. For example, Niemi et al. (1983) use survey data to explore the reasons people give for not voting. In an open-ended question, abstainers never cite poll results as a reason for their nonparticipation. When asked to evaluate the importance of possible reasons for not turning out, some abstainers rate "the polls showed the candidates I liked were too far behind" or "the polls showed the candidates I liked were way ahead" as very or somewhat important motivations, but overall, polling results were the least popular reason chosen for abstaining. Analysing the 1972–2000 American National Election Studies (ANES), Giammo (2004) finds that the likelihood of voting is significantly higher among individuals who perceive that the election is going to be close during the campaign survey, though these perceptions are weakly connected to the tightness of polling margins prior to the date of interview. Leveraging variation in the availability of poll results and their prominence in media coverage during Swiss referenda, Bursztyn and colleagues (2017) conclude that polls signalling tight contests stimulate aggregate turnout while those signalling large margins decrease participation, especially when polls receive more media attention.

Experiments conducted during real campaigns also produce mixed results. In some instances, providing polling information signalling close or lopsided races affects willingness to vote for subsets of the treatment groups (de Bock 1976; Biggers et al. 2017). However, no significant effect of poll closeness on voter turnout is discovered in a television-based lab experiment (Ansolabehere and Iyengar 1994) or a large-scale field experiment (Gerber et al. 2020).[5] In contrast, lab experiments using economic voting games among undergraduate students suggest poll closeness boosts participation (Großer and Schram 2010; Klor and Winter 2017; Agranov et al. 2018). Given the variation in the findings across studies, the evidence about the impact of the competitiveness of the race portrayed by opinion polls on electoral participation remains uncertain.

The third and arguably more dominant strand of poll research concerns the influence of opinion polls on the choice of voters. This work considers whether

---

[4] Blais put it rather bluntly: "This is the most firmly established result in the literature. I cannot see how this finding could be wrong" (2006: 119).

[5] Other experimental studies of the impact of race closeness on turnout did not explicitly rely on information communicated by public opinion polls (e.g., Gerber and Green 2000; Bennion 2005; Dale and Straus 2009; Enos and Fowler 2014). Their findings are also mixed.

exposure to polling results during campaigns makes people vote differently on election day than they would have absent polling information. There are two main arguments regarding how poll information may affect the ballot that is cast: a bandwagon effect, where people rally toward the frontrunner, and an underdog effect, where voters flock to a second-place challenger (Simon 1954). While many studies record notable effects of polls on vote choice, there is no consensus about the nature, or direction, of these effects. Some researchers point to a bandwagon effect. Some find the opposite pattern, an underdog effect. Others uncover no effect at all.

A number of observational studies offer results that are consistent with the bandwagon effect, but they do not necessarily imply a direct impact of polls. For instance, an analysis of US primary elections by Bartels (1985) reports a positive link between expectations about the candidates' chances of winning and voting preferences during the early portion of the campaign.[6] Similar findings are identified in an American presidential campaign (Gimpel and Harvey 1997) and a German national election (Schmitt-Beck 1996). Using the 1980 ANES, Skalaban (1988) finds that people who said they had been following the polls and watching television news were more likely to vote for Ronald Reagan, the candidate leading in the polls. In exit polls administered during the 1979–1987 British elections, McAllister and Studlar (1991) ascertain that respondents who knew the Conservatives are leading in the polls were more prone to vote for that party (while controlling for partisanship). Some research on the consequences of early election outcome announcements for voting behaviour in later time zones also suggests the existence of a bandwagon effect (Delli Carpini 1984; Morton et al. 2015). In addition, a regression discontinuity design applied to 26 French runoff elections shows that candidates who narrowly finish higher in the first round have a better chance of winning in the second round than those who narrowly finish lower, a pattern consistent with bandwagoning (Pons and Tricaud 2019). More convincing for the relevance of polls, combining an intricate content analysis and a two-wave panel survey in Germany, Stolwijk, Schuck, and de Vreese (2017) conclude that exposure to poll reports favourable toward a party positively affects the likelihood of voting for that party.

There is also evidence of the bandwagon effect from controlled experiments. Presenting the results of the 1936 Literary Digest straw poll increased the

---

[6] While polling results seem to affect expectations (e.g., Johnston et al. 1992; Irwin and van Holsteyn 2002; Blais and Bodet 2006), other factors are also relevant, notably projection or "wishful thinking". Bartels' subsequent work abandons the use of the term bandwagon to describe this expectations-vote relationship and adopts the term "momentum" instead (Bartels 1987, 1988).

proportion of college students preferring Alf Landon over Franklin Roosevelt, though not by a statistically significant margin (Cook and Welch 1940). Embedding a poll story in a televised news broadcast leads to higher proportions of people willing to vote for the candidate leading the presidential, senatorial or mayoral race (Ansolabehere and Iyengar 1994). Poll results delivered in written format induce movement in national vote intentions as well: the parties portrayed as gaining ground in the polls obtained more support in both Denmark (Dahlgaard et al. 2017) and the Netherlands (van der Meer, Hakhverdian, and Aaldering 2016). Non-electoral studies also uncover bandwagon behaviour toward the majority's opinions in Canada, Germany and the United States using survey experiments regarding divisive issues such as abortion and Quebec sovereignty (Marsh 1985; Nadeau, Cloutier, and Guay 1993; Rothschild and Malhotra 2014) and economic voting games about the selection of an organisation for a monetary donation (Bischoff and Egbert 2013; Farjam forthcoming).

However, while less common, there are studies that report the presence of an underdog effect. Two observational studies comparing polls from early in the campaign to election day results in the UK over three decades (Sanders 2003) and in Australia over ten elections (Goot 2010) highlight the less popular party gaining support during the campaign. In an experimental study, Fleitas (1971) finds that polling information does not sway undergraduate subjects, but information about the financial resources of fictitious candidates shifts support toward the underdog. Participants in a student-populated experiment that involved two separate exposures to polling results tended to change their voting intentions in favour of the frontrunner following the first manipulation but away from the frontrunner after the second manipulation (Ceci and Kain 1982). Another set of experimental studies that capture pre- and post-treatment opinion measurements discover the existence of divergent individual reactions: a bandwagon effect for some people and an underdog effect for others (Cloutier, Nadeau, and Guay 1989; Chung, Heo, and Moon 2018). Finally, a set of non-electoral experiments indicates that students have a tendency to express greater support for the underdog in a sporting competition or an international conflict when they do not have well-defined prior opinions (Vandello, Goldschied, and Richards 2007).

Other studies obtain null or minimal effects of polls on individuals' voting behaviour. People who say they heard or read polling results during the last month did not have different presidential voting preferences in the 1980 ANES compared to those who were not exposed to pre-election polling information (West 1991). Examining Gallup polls of American presidential campaigns between 1936 and 1972, Beniger (1976) shows that the leading candidate in a given poll was not more likely to gain (or lose) support in the subsequent poll. Looking at the impact on vote choice of changes in polling results between panel waves across four decades of the ANES, Giammo (2004) unearths no significant relationship. Blais, Vowles, and Aarts (2002) further conclude there is no connection between published polls and vote intentions in rolling cross-sectional election studies in Canada, the Netherlands, and New Zealand (while controlling for time trends). Similarly, Blais, Gidengil, and Nevitte (2006) find neither a bandwagon nor an underdog effect in the rolling cross-sectional 1988 Canadian Election Study. Using experimental approaches, Fleitas (1971), as mentioned previously, and Daschmann (2000) both fail to reveal poll effects on vote intentions.

These conflicting and null findings may come about because the impact of polls on voting is inconsistent, conditional upon individuals' characteristics and/or contextual factors. For example, Navazio (1977), using an experimental design, discerns no significant overall effect of poll exposure, but detects a bandwagon effect among white-collar workers and an underdog effect among blue-collar workers. Both Cloutier et al. (1989) and Chung et al. (2018) show that a single poll generates contrary reactions among different individuals: some people rally behind the leader, while others flock toward the challenger. According to analyses by Binning and colleagues (2015), poll effects on frontrunner support are conditional on sense of personal integrity and sense of national identity. Also, Stolwijk et al. (2017) describe how emotions, such as anxiety and enthusiasm, mediate the impact of polls. With regard to issue attitudes (toward troops in Afghanistan, free trade, and public financing of elections), Rothschild and Malhotra (2014) uncover evidence of bandwagon effects, though their magnitude depends on the issue in question. Additionally, van der Meer et al. (2016) determine that the extent to which polls engender bandwagoning is contingent upon whether the results are accompanied by a short account that frames a party as gaining support.

Research examining the impact of poll exposure on vote choice has also considered whether polls foster strategic voting by providing people the information they need about the viability of election competitors to choose tactically (e.g., Blais and Bodet 2006).[7] Indeed, without information on parties' relative support levels, casting a meaningful strategic vote would not be possible. Knowledge of poll standings can lead a voter to abandon a hopeless preferred party in favour of a more viable alternative to defeat the most disliked option. Or, it can lead one to switch support to a party that is very near clearing a statutory electoral threshold or becoming a viable partner in a governing coalition.

---

[7] Blais and Bodet (2006) show that dynamics in party support signalled by published polls are a significant predictor of citizens' assessments of the parties' chances of winning during the 1988 Canadian election campaign.

A number of studies reveal evidence of a positive effect of poll exposure on strategic voting. Using Gallup exit polls, McAllister and Studlar (1991) find that respondents who claim to have been influenced by the polls and decided which party to support during the campaign are more inclined to vote Alliance in the 1983 and 1987 UK elections, a pattern the authors deem consistent with tactical voting. Burden (2005) shows that, in the 2000 American presidential election, support for third-place Ralph Nader decreased when the polls indicated a closer race between the two main contenders. In the 1988 Canadian Election Study rolling cross-section, campaign vote intentions for the second- and third-place parties in a three-way race are swayed by the gap between those two parties in public polls (despite taking leader and party evaluations into account): some opponents of the frontrunner appear to converge on the more viable contender (Blais et al. 2006). Relying on experiments with mock three-candidate plurality elections with assigned preferences, Merolla (2009) observes that American participants randomly exposed to polling results are more likely to vote for their second favourite candidate when he or she is depicted by polls to be more viable than their favourite candidate. With an analogous research design, Rich (2015) also finds that strategic voting increases as support for the third-place candidate decreases in the polls. Based on lab experiments conducted during an actual election campaign with real party preferences under Germany's mixed-member proportional system, Meffert and Gschwend (2011) report that exposure to polls heralding a close race near the threshold for parliamentary entry encourages strategic voting, such as shifting from a large preferred party for the benefit of a small potential coalition partner. Survey experiments conducted within Sweden's proportional electoral system exhibit comparable findings (Freden 2017). However, a recent survey experiment in the context of a Canadian election by Blais and colleagues (2018) fails to substantiate the idea that polling information affects strategic voting among persons with a clear incentive to desert a top choice with little chance of winning, and this null finding holds across levels of voter interest and optimism.

Finally, there are some indications from laboratory voting games among students that polls improve the 'quality' of vote decisions. Poll exposure raises the likelihood that one will vote for the ideologically nearest candidate (Sinclair and Plott 2012), and it reduces the likelihood of victory for the Condorcet loser—the candidate that would lose all two-way races (Forsythe et al. 1993).

1.2. Theoretical Grounding and Hypotheses

While the review above recognizes the extensive body of literature that already exists pertaining to the influence of polls on voting behaviour and preferences, we believe that the work to date has largely overlooked an important aspect of poll effects: whether exposure to polling results affects how citizens engage with election information. In what follows, we aim to address this gap in the literature by considering how poll exposure shapes the amount of information voters gather during an election campaign. We then build upon prior research to examine the impact of poll exposure on vote choice. For both information search and vote choice, we take into account factors that could condition the effects of polls: individual-level characteristics as well as poll content and mode of presentation.

Election campaigns provide an opportunity for citizens to spend time researching the relevant issues, learning candidates' positions on these issues, and deliberating over the qualifications of the candidates to handle them competently. However, most citizens do not accomplish these tasks. There is abundant evidence that the average voter has little interest in politics, pays little attention to campaigns, and possesses little knowledge about the issues and candidates (Berelson, Lazarsfeld, and McPhee 1954; Converse 1964; Luskin 1987; Delli Carpini and Keeter 1996; Gidengil et al. 2004). While political knowledge, or the lack thereof, is heavily dependent on socioeconomic and intrinsic factors (Luskin 1990; Delli Carpini and Keeter 1996), extrinsic political circumstances can substantially affect information levels. These include women's representation in legislatures (Fraile and Gomez 2017; Dassonneville and McAllister 2018), the character of party systems (Gordon and Segura 1997; Fraile and Gomez 2017), and electoral system (dis)proportionality (Gordon and Segura 1997; Kittilson and Schwindt-Bayer 2010). To this list, we add public opinion polls.

What effect should polls have on the amount of attention citizens pay to election information? First, there is a rationale for expecting that polls showing a close race could prompt a more comprehensive search for information. Kam and Utych (2011) argue that close elections generate greater cognitive engagement and information seeking among citizens for three reasons: the larger perceived chance of casting a pivotal vote increases the motivation to be accurate, group-based loyalties are activated, along with the desire to root for your party, and the uncertainty of the outcome makes for a good spectacle that can engender interest and curiosity. All three reasons can inspire people to gather more information about the competitors. In fact, the observational and experimental findings of Kam and Utych (2011; Utych and Kam 2014) show that the closeness of the race and candidate viability are associated with more information seeking, knowledge acquisition, and election news recall.

However, polls should not routinely indicate close races, because election results are not routinely close. For example, in US post-war presidential elections through 2020, the average margin of victory in the popular vote is just under eight percentage points.[8] In UK general elections during this period, the average margin between the first-place party and the runner-up is six points.[9] And, in both countries, constituency-level results tend to be even more lopsided.

Our expectation is that exposure to polling results will reduce the amount of effort that voters devote to searching for campaign information—and not only because polls do not regularly indicate close races. The argument is based on the following logic. Citizens can rely on uncomplicated information cues, such as party labels and endorsements, to simplify the arduous process of deliberation (Popkin 1991; Sniderman, Brody, and Tetlock 1991; Lupia 1994; Kam 2005; Arceneaux and Kolodny 2009; Nicholson 2012; Laustsen and Petersen 2016). This paradigm comes under many labels: notably heuristic processing, peripheral processing, low-information rationality, and system 1 thinking (Kam 2005; Kahneman 2011). Public opinion polls can also be construed as cues that citizens may use as shortcuts for processing the political environment (McKelvey and Ordeshook 1985; Bartels 1988; Popkin 1991; Mutz 1992, 1998; Schmitt-Beck 1996; Lau and Redlawsk 2001; Boudreau and McCubbins 2010; Meffert and Gschwend 2011). By summarizing the electorate's perceptions about the competing parties' strengths and weaknesses, polls provide a quick-and-easy indicator of the popularity of the various alternatives according to the judgement of other people.

The key is that polling cues can have an impact on the cognitive workload of the decision-making process (Lau and Redlawsk 2001: 953–954). Citizens may take advantage of the signals provided by polls to reduce the burden of decision-making. Polls can simplify voters' deliberation by limiting the set of alternatives that are considered to only the most viable options. They can thus help citizens avoid wasting time and energy gathering information about competitors that have no chance of winning. If voters are the "cognitive misers" envisioned by Fiske and Taylor (1991), then they will rationally disinvest time and effort spent on learning about the competing options when given cues that allows them to do so. As such, individuals who are exposed to polls should lessen the amount of information they accumulate during campaigns.

In contrast, when they are not privy to polling results, citizens have a larger incentive to seek out information on the competing candidates or parties. This may involve reading the news, watching leaders' debates, having political discussions, and a number of additional avenues for getting informed. Of course, those who are exposed to polls are not precluded from such activities—and many

---

[8] We calculated this using data from: https://uselectionatlas.org/.
[9] We calculated this using data from: https://researchbriefings.parliament.uk/.

of them may indeed continue gathering information. We simply believe the incentives are less widespread when polls are available. And the prominence of polling results in contemporary media coverage of election campaigns means that these cues are easily and extensively available.

As such, we expect that one effect of polls will be to decrease the search for electoral information. We thus put forth our first hypothesis:

H1a: Exposure to polls will reduce information seeking.

But our argument also makes clear that the effect of polls on the information search should be mediated by the party standings. Our assumption is that parties shown to be at the back of the pack will receive even less attention when their weak support is primed by poll results relative to the attention the same parties receive absent polling information. In other words, voters should particularly disregard parties that have no plausible chance of winning the election. Accordingly, we specify:

H1b: Exposure to polls will reduce information seeking, especially for parties trailing in the polls.

We also re-examine the longstanding concerns about whether polling results lead people to vote differently than how they would have without access to information on the competitors' standings. Beyond affecting the cognitive workload, polling cues can also influence vote choice (e.g., McKelvey and Ordeshook 1985; Meffert and Gschwend 2011). Knowing about the relative public support of the electoral contestants can help people decide how to vote. Indeed, the aforementioned literature on the link between polls and strategic voting suggests that some voters do make rational use of the information they are provided when casting a ballot. Yet, given the inconclusive nature of prior research about the impact of polls on vote choice, we believe that further investigating this research question constitutes a worthwhile endeavour. Vote choice thus serves as this project's second core dependent variable. As we note in the previous sub-section, evidence of a bandwagon effect is more common than evidence of an underdog effect. While we recognize that some people rally behind the second-place challenger, we believe they are outnumbered by those who move toward the frontrunner. Such a conclusion emerges from a study that simultaneously measures bandwagon and underdog behaviour with experimental panel data on pre-existing political preferences (Cloutier et al. 1989). Various psychological mechanisms have been proposed as explanations for bandwagoning behaviour, notably: conformity to group norms (Marsh 1985: 71), emotional contagion or a herd instinct (Bartels 1988: 111), gratification from backing a winner (Bartels 1988: 112), a strategic response to differences in viability (Bartels 1988: 109), a consensus heuristic regarding the quality of the alternatives (Mutz 1992: 97), self-persuasion through mental rehearsals of arguments (Mutz 1992: 98), and succumbing to inevitability (Kenney and Rice 1994: 925). The process can be either conscious or unconscious (McAllister and Studlar 1991: 721). We remain agnostic about which mechanism (or set of mechanisms) is valid. Regardless of the reasons why people do so, we anticipate that poll exposure fosters bandwagon voting. So, our second hypothesis states:

H2a: Exposure to polls will increase the likelihood of voting for the lead party.

Although we expect the dominant reaction to polls to be the bandwagon effect when it comes to vote choice, our empirical analyses will nevertheless explicitly test for an underdog effect, and we will gauge the impact of polls on strategic desertion. We anticipate that exposure to poll information will deter voting for parties shown to be trailing. As we summarised previously, evidence that polling information encourages voters to abandon candidates and parties with little chance of being elected in plurality elections is quite robust (e.g., Burden 2005; Blais et al. 2006; Merolla 2009; Rich 2015), but it is not unanimous (e.g., Blais et al. 2018). Of course, strategic desertion and bandwagon/underdog effects are not necessarily at odds, they can be connected logically. Within the context of a first-past-the-post system, one could even see strategic desertion as an antecedent of the other two effects: citizens may first learn about the potential of wasting their vote on a hopeless option and then choose to switch their vote to a more viable contender in first or second place, thereby producing bandwagon and underdog effects respectively.[10] Hence, we assert:

H2b: Exposure to polls will decrease the likelihood of voting for parties trailing in the polls.

However, poll effects on the information search and vote choice should not be uniform. Several sources of heterogeneity should moderate the impacts of polls: individual-level characteristics, poll content, and poll presentation. We begin with three individual-level factors.

Partisanship should matter. Some people have a psychological attachment to a political party, others do not (Campbell et al. 1960; Green, Palmquist, and Schickler 2004). The latter group represents much more fertile ground for poll effects than the former. Party identifiers are more likely to remain loyal and to

---

[10] Note, these paths do not offer an exhaustive list. For instance, some bandwagoners could also come from the ranks of the second-place party supporters.

vote for "their" party, regardless of what happens during the campaign (Bartels 2000; Gidengil et al. 2012; Dassonneville forthcoming). Partisanship also colours and biases perceptions of reality and information processing (Bartels 2002; Gaines et al. 2007; Gerber, Huber, and Washington 2010; Tilley and Hobolt 2011; Jerit and Barabas 2012; Mitchell 2012; Achen and Bartels 2017; Bisgaard and Slothuus 2018). Because partisans are less volatile and less prone to update their beliefs when confronting new evidence, the effects of polling results on the information search and vote choice should be more muted among this group.

Conversely, non-partisans should exhibit stronger poll effects. Being less committed to a particular party, more open to adjusting their attitudes, and in greater need of decisional shortcuts, non-partisans ought to be more likely to respond to the cues provided by polling results. For instance, Mitchell (2012) finds that independents tend to modify their evaluation of a candidate according to information circulating during a lab experiment to a larger extent than those who identify with that candidate's party.[11] We predict:

H3a: Exposure to polls will reduce information seeking, especially for non-partisans.

H3b: Exposure to polls will increase the likelihood of voting for the lead party, especially for non-partisans.

We next consider political sophistication. This concept refers to the size, range, and organisation of a person's political belief system (Luskin 1987). It is traditionally measured by the accuracy of answers to factual knowledge questions about politics (Luskin 1987; Delli Carpini and Keeter 1993; Mondak 2001; Barabas et al. 2014). It is correlated with a number of potentially desirable election-related outcomes, including precise perceptions of party positions and economic conditions (Tilley, Garry, and Bold 2008; Fortunato and Stevenson 2013; Alt, Marshall, and Lassen 2016; Aldrich et al. 2018; Carroll and Kubo 2018), electoral turnout (Delli Carpini and Keeter 1996; Lassen 2005; Larcinese 2007; Fischer et al. 2008; Smets and van Ham 2013), and voting for the most proximate party (Lau, Andersen, and Redlawsk 2008; Lau et al. 2014; Tomz and Van Houweling 2008; Jessee 2009, 2010). More importantly, sophistication is frequently identified as a source of interpersonal heterogeneity in political cognition and behaviour, notably in decision-making (Sniderman, Brody and Tetlock 1991; Zaller, 1992; Johnston et al. 1996; Fournier 2006; Roy 2011), the influence of contextual factors (Bosch and Orriols 2014; Mayne and Hakhverdian 2017), media effects (Krosnick and Brannon 1993; Miller and

---

[11] Though partisanship does not appear to moderate the relationship between polls and perceived chances of winning (Blais and Bodet 2006).

Krosnick 2000; Druckman and Nelson 2003; Soroka et al. 2016; Fournier, Cutler, and Soroka 2019), and vote choice (Bartels 1996; Oscarsson 2007; Blais et al. 2009; Hansen 2009; Bhatti 2010; Arnold 2012; Fowler and Margolis 2014; Rapeli 2018).

How should sophistication interact with the influence of polls? Citizens with high levels of sophistication tend to undertake a more detailed vote decision calculus (Johnston et al. 1996; Roy 2011; Singh and Roy 2014) and to place more emphasis on ideological and issue-relevant considerations (Delli Carpini and Keeter 1996; Sniderman et al. 1991; Lau and Redlawsk 2001; Kam 2005; Jacoby 2009; Federico and Hunt 2013). Because they rely less on ideology and policy substance, it seems reasonable to assume that individuals with low levels of sophistication are more prone to use cues and shortcuts (such as polls) when deciding how to vote.

However, while sophistication moderates reliance on cues, it does not do so in a consistent and straightforward way. The link between sophistication and cues varies by the sort of shortcut. The types of cues can be divided into three broad categories. First, some cues are very simple, easily accessible, and deliver instant inferences (Sniderman, Brody, and Tetlock 1991). These cues are more likely to be employed by the less sophisticated. For instance, affective reactions toward well-known groups such as Black people and homosexuals are stronger drivers of opinions regarding government policies directed at those groups among the less educated (Sniderman et al. 1991: 31–69).

Second, some cues are more complex and require higher levels of attention and understanding of the political environment to be useful. They are therefore more commonly used by the more sophisticated. For example, when Canadians faced a national referendum on a complex constitutional reform proposal in 1992, an intervention by former prime minister Pierre Trudeau denouncing the proposal had an immediate and decisive impact on public support for it (Johnston et al. 1996). But, the voters who were aware of the intervention, who knew Trudeau's position, and who connected this to the vote were the well informed, not those who most needed help (the poorly informed). Another illustration is the likability heuristic (Sniderman et al. 1991). It allows a person to infer the stance of a politically-relevant group (e.g., conservatives) concerning an issue (e.g., abortion) on the basis of two elements: the person's personal position on the issue and the person's affective evaluation of the group. In a nutshell, if you like the group, then you expect that it shares your opinion (and vice-versa). Because it requires coherent pre-existing beliefs and feelings, the likability heuristic is more prevalent among those more attentive to politics.

Third, some cues mobilize a sense of social identity and belonging to a key reference group, and they tend to generate motivated reasoning as a defence mechanism that biases information processing in order to protect cherished affiliations (Malka and Lelkes 2010; Slothuus and de Vreese 2010; Kahan 2012; Lodge and Taber 2013; Petersen et al. 2013; Bakker, Lelkes, and Malka 2020). Such thinking is more typical of the highly sophisticated. For instance, experimental work by Slothuus and de Vreese (2010) and Bakker and colleagues (2020) shows that partisans with greater political knowledge are more likely to modify their policy opinions when exposed to the political parties' positions on those issues.

So, where do poll cues fit within these three categories? Given that such cues are widely circulated and contain a rather simple message from a (typically) non-partisan source, we believe that individuals with lower levels of political sophistication will be more affected by poll exposure. That is, the less sophisticated should be especially likely to reduce their information gathering and to rally behind the frontrunner when exposed to polls. Correspondingly, prior studies of polls provide some evidence that their effects are more pronounced among the less educated (Schmitt- Beck 1996), the less cognisant of an issue (Johnston et al. 1996; Boudreau and McCubbins 2010), and the less informed about politics (Meffert and Gschwend 2011).[12] Even though politically knowledgeable voters are more prone to consume polling results, their probability of voting strategically is less influenced by polls (Meffert and Gschwend 2011). Consequently, we propose:

H4a: Exposure to polls will reduce information seeking, especially for those who are less politically sophisticated.

H4b: Exposure to polls will increase the likelihood of voting for the lead party, especially for those who are less politically sophisticated.

The level of confidence that people have in public opinion polls should also condition the impacts of polls on the information search and vote choice. Quite simply, if you do not trust polls or deem them to be biased and/or inaccurate, you are unlikely to give much credence to their signals or to change your attitudes and behaviours in reaction to them. Inversely, if you consider polls reliable reflections of public opinion, you are more prone to be swayed by the cues they provide. Indeed, extant research shows a robust link between source credibility/ trustworthiness and persuasion (e.g., Hovland and Weiss 1951; Petty and Wegener 1998; Miller and Krosnick 2000; Druckman 2001; Pornpitakpan 2004; Ismagilova et al. 2020). Therefore:

---

[12] Null findings on the moderating role of education are reported by van der Meer et al. (2016), and contrary results on information are reported by Blais and Bodet (2006).

H5a: Exposure to polls will reduce information seeking, especially for individuals with higher levels of confidence in polls.

H5b: Exposure to polls will increase the likelihood of voting for the lead party, especially for individuals with higher levels of confidence in polls.

Beyond individual-level characteristics, we also expect that the nature of the information conveyed by the polls should influence the magnitude of their effects. Exploring these dimensions will not only help us better understand the conditions under which polls are consequential, it has the potential to shed light on the contradictions and discrepancies in previous research; perhaps prior studies uncover divergent results because they use different polling stimuli.

We first consider the level of election competitiveness conveyed by polls. If public opinion polls provide cues that voters draw upon when deliberating about the electoral competitors and how to cast their ballot, polls that convey a clear frontrunner, as indicated by a large gap between the first- and second-place parties, should be more effectual. A lopsided race should lead to a diminished information search. When the outcome seems a foregone conclusion and citizens perceive that their vote cannot make a difference, they are unlikely to be interested in the election and motivated to gather information about the competing candidates and parties (Kam and Utych 2011). Indeed, as we discuss in the previous sub-section, various studies document that a closer race revealed by campaign polls raises turnout or the willingness to vote (de Bock 1976; Giammo 2004; Großer and Schram 2010; Biggers et al. 2017; Bursztyn et al. 2017; Klor and Winter 2017; Agranov et al. 2018). Moreover, Kam and Utych (2011; Utych and Kam 2014) show that a tighter contest enhances cognitive engagement.

With regard to vote choice, a race with a runaway leader should encourage bandwagon voting. When the consensus of the population materializes unambiguously behind a particular competitor, the social pressure to rally toward the favourite is amplified. As Ansolabehere and Iyengar (1994: 425) note: "the more favorable the poll information, the more significant the surge in electoral support for the candidate leading in the polls". A similar link between the level of public backing for an option in polls and support for that option is reported in the work of Bischoff and Egbert (2013) and Rothschild and Malhotra (2014).

Accordingly, regarding the competitiveness of the race reflected in polls, we expect the following:

H6a: Exposure to polls will reduce information seeking, especially when the gap between the lead and second-place party is larger.

H6b: Exposure to polls will increase the likelihood of voting for the lead party, especially when the gap between the lead and second-place party is larger.

We next consider whether citizens' capacity for understanding polling results regulates the impacts of polls. There are mounting concerns over the public's level of numeracy—knowledge and skills related to the comprehension and use of quantitative information (Paulos 1988; Lipkus, Samsa, and Rimer. 2001; Kutner et al. 2006; Rayna et al. 2009; Craig 2018). Individual differences in numeracy are notably associated with framing effects (Peters et al. 2006; Peters and Levin 2008), risk perceptions (Dieckmann, Slovic, and Peters 2009; Hart 2013), financial wealth (Lusardi and Mitchell 2007; Estrada-Mejia, De Vries, and Zeelenberg 2016), health decisions and outcomes (Schwartz et al. 1997; Cavanaugh et al. 2008; Apter et al. 2009), and ideology (Choma, Sumantry, and Hanoch 2019). There is even evidence that numeracy moderates political persuasion: the impact of quantitative policy messages is driven by strength of argument rather than partisan cues among those high in numeracy, while the reverse is true among the less numerate (Mérola and Hitt 2016).

Polling information can be presented with numbers and graphs, or it can be described with words. Quantitative presentations, however simple they may be, could prove difficult to grasp for innumerate segments of the population. This implies that poll results might be more influential when they are delivered in a non-quantitative fashion. In fact, there are some indications of this in the study by van der Meer, Hakhverdian, and Aaldering (2016), where the only significant bandwagon effect emerges when the treatment contains a short passage stressing that a party in fourth place has recently picked up support. We will ascertain whether the impacts of public opinion polls on the information search and vote choice differ when the polling content appears as a graph or as text. Our final hypotheses are:

H7a: Exposure to polls will reduce information seeking, especially when polling results are conveyed by text.

H7b: Exposure to polls will increase the likelihood of voting for the lead party, especially when polling results are conveyed by text.

We turn now to our empirical strategy to measure the impact of poll exposure on information seeking and vote choice.

1.3. Our Empirical Strategy

Since our research questions about the influence of public opinion polls include the moderating role of respondent characteristics, we need individual-level data. We are reluctant to employ observational data for this particular investigation. Self-reports about the factors that explain respondents' behaviour (e.g., Niemi et al. 1983) are untrustworthy. Correlations between reported poll exposure and behaviour (e.g., Skalaban 1988; West 1991) are bound to be fraught with omitted variable bias, as numerous factors affect both poll attention and political behaviour, as well as reverse causality. Even when observational studies rely on a seemingly more objective indicator of poll exposure, such as date of interview (e.g., Blais et al. 2002; 2006), it is difficult to be confident that a correlation between the publication of a poll and citizen behaviour means that people are actually reacting to the polling information about the parties' standings, rather than simply reacting to the parties' campaign performance, to media coverage of the campaign, or to other events that occurred on the same day as the poll's release.

Randomized experimental studies can provide greater certainty about the isolation of the impact of polling information, making it the only element to differ between control and treatment groups. However, greater internal validity often comes at the price of lower external validity (McDermott 2011). The main concern regarding polling experiments is the risk of artificiality. When experiments include fictional elections and ignore pre-existing preferences, we fear that the estimates of poll influence are inflated and implausible. Even the results of experiments with real party preferences can be exaggerated and unbelievable if the poll manipulations are excessive and beyond the realm of possible opinion dynamics. Further, experimental results detected among samples that differ substantially from the population in which one is interested, such as those composed of university undergraduates, may not generalize well.

Therefore, our approach is to rely on realistic experiments with representative samples. With the exception of the experimental treatments designed to test the impact of the size of the lead conveyed in polls, we use real political parties, real party attachments, and actual poll standings at the time of fieldwork.[13] Moreover, we have evidence from ten independent studies conducted across six countries on four continents: Argentina, Australia, Canada, New Zealand, United Kingdom (England only), and the United States. To our knowledge, this represents the most broadly comparative experimental study of poll effects to date.

Drawing on this extensive experimental research, this book provides a timely empirical evaluation of the impact polls have on both the vote decision process and vote choice. We explore not only how polls affect the voting choices

---

[13] After presenting our main results, we also examine whether the use of actual versus artificial party labels influences treatment effects.

individuals make, but also the ways in which they arrive at these decisions, along with the types of individuals that are most susceptible to such effects.

1.4. Outline of the Book

Section 2 provides a full description of the experimental platform and the ten studies used in this work, including variation across studies that allow us to assess the impact of polls and how poll effects may vary according to both individual- and poll-level aspects. It also describes our sampling technique and data cleaning process. We then discuss the measurement of our core dependent and independent variables, and report the summary statistics for all studies. Finally, we present our approach to parameter estimation and the presentation of results.

Section 3 is the first of two results sections. It tackles the impact of polls on the information search. We directly assess one of our key research questions: does exposure to polling information affect how much information people access when deciding how to vote and the amount of time they spend doing so? We then dissect these results, considering how the effects vary according to individual- and poll-level factors.

Section 4 examines the impact of poll exposure on vote choice. We test for bandwagon effects (rallying behind the frontrunner), underdog effects (flocking to a second-place contender), and strategic desertion (abandoning an option with no chance of winning in favour of a more viable option). We once again present the results of overall effects first, followed by a full assessment of conditional effects according to individual- and poll-level characteristics.

Our final section offers a summary of our findings, along with an assessment of how well our results fit within the existing literature and their implications for electoral policy. We use this concluding section to discuss the strengths and weaknesses of our design and results. We also consider avenues for future research, both as a means of testing the robustness of our work and as a way to further advance the understanding of how polls influence political behaviour and preferences.

2. Methodology and Measurement

With observational research, estimates of the effects of exposure to public opinion polls on information seeking, our first dependent variable, are threatened by two main sources of endogeneity. First, it is likely that individuals who choose to view or are exposed to polls are already predisposed to be information seekers. Second, exposure to polls and information seeking are likely mutually related to a number of factors, not all of which can be detected, measured, and taken into account. Similar challenges relate to the impact that polls may have on vote choice: individuals who are prone to voting in a particular way are perhaps more likely to see polls, and omitted variable bias may confound the estimated relationships between poll exposure and changes in voting behaviour. Further, any reliance on self-reported polling effects would be fraught with difficulties, as there is a strong possibility that individuals may not be aware of the impact that polls have on their decisions. Thus, the usual tool for the study of public opinion and voting behaviour— a survey—is problematic when trying to ascertain whether exposure to polls influences information seeking and the vote that is cast. Accordingly, as we explain in the previous section, we contend that the most effective way to study poll effects is to use an experimental design.

Our experiments are conducted within an online election simulation, which allows us to credibly measure how much effort participants invest into the decision-making process and to capture their vote choices directly. We randomize poll exposure and then compare differences in the information seeking process and vote preferences due to the availability of polling results. This helps us overcome the problems inherent to survey research on polling effects stemming from endogeneity and self-reports.

2.1. The Studies

We administered our experiments in Argentina (February-March 2018), Australia (April 2016), Canada (February 2014; March 2016; March 2017; July 2020), England (March 2016), New Zealand (May 2016), and the United States (May 2018; October-November 2018), for a total of ten independent studies.[14] The countries differ in terms of culture, history, electoral and party systems, and the design of democratic institutions. This variation allows us to assess whether polling effects are sensitive to such contextual variation: similar findings in each of the countries would suggest that macro-level factors do not condition the influence of polls.[15]

---

[14] As the competing parties and alliances differ across Argentinian provinces, we restricted our sample to Buenos Aires Province, which accounts for nearly 40 percent of the country's population. We excluded Quebec, which has a unique party system, from the Canadian samples. Quebec accounts for just under a quarter of the Canadian population. We restricted our study to England due to party system differences across the United Kingdom. In the US, we administered one study six months prior to the 2018 mid-term elections and the second in the final two weeks of the election campaign. We refer to the latter study as "United States 2018 (Nov.)" even though the study was in the field for the last week of October as well.

[15] While the cross-national variation across cases allows for a general assessment of the robustness of our results to different cultural, historical, and electoral settings, we do not have the statistical power necessary to introduce the controls needed to assess how macro-level factors may influence poll effects. The inclusion of Argentina, which may appear as somewhat of an outlier, is a reflection of our desire to include at least one case that differed from the highly developed

To populate our studies, we hired Dynata, a private international firm that specializes in online sampling and surveying. Participants were incentivized to complete the study as part of Dynata's reward program, which offers points for completed surveys that can be exchanged for prizes through an online market-place, as well as entry into a quarterly prize draw.[16] Sampling was performed within strata for gender, age, education, and household income to ensure the sample was reflective of the population along these characteristics. We instructed Dynata to gather samples of approximately 2,000 to 2,500 partici-pants in each study. We obtained approval from the Research Ethics Board of Wilfrid Laurier University in Ontario, Canada, before beginning our research, and all participants gave consent before participating.[17]

After completing a pre-experiment survey, participants were randomly assigned to either a control group or an experimental group.[18] Random assign-ment was achieved via a computer script that generated a random number for each participant. All participants received a brief set of instructions that wel-comed them to an online election and explained that they would be presented with information on the four largest nationally competitive political parties—or, in Argentina, alliances of parties.[19] Participants were told that they could view information for each party or alliance by clicking on the title of the information link that they wished to see. The final set of instructions stated: "Once you have viewed enough information to make your decision, click on the 'Next' button located on the bottom of the election campaign screen to cast your ballot".

For the Australia, Canada 2014 and 2016, England, and New Zealand studies, the information pertained to each party's position on the economy, the environ-ment, democratic reform, employment, and social policy. The Canada 2014 study included a sixth information link outlining each party's position on foreign affairs. For the Argentina, Canada 2017 and 2020, and two US studies, participants were able to access information on the parties' or alliances' posi-tions on the economy and the environment, an endorsement for each party,[20]

Anglo-American democracies of Australia, Canada (sans Quebec), New Zealand, the United Kingdom (England only), and the United States

[16] Dynata was formerly called Survey Sampling International. See http://www.dynata.com for information about the panel and rewards program.

[17] WLU Research Ethics Board approval, file #4819.

[18] The pre-experiment survey included socio-demographic characteristics, personality traits, political knowledge and interest, as well as opinion questions for all studies run in 2014–2016. For studies conducted after 2016, the pre-experiment survey was similar, apart from the fact that the socio-demographic questions were asked at the end of the study, after the respondent had expressed their vote choice. See Online Appendix 2.1 for details on the questions asked in each study.

[19] The instruction screen for each study is available in Online Appendix 2.2.

[20] In Argentina and the US, for each alliance or party, respectively, the endorsement links merely contained a message stating that no endorsement was available.

and non-policy information in the form of party leader photos, party leader biographies, and broad party campaign statements (which tended to be more platitudinous than policy-based). All of the information was accurate and drawn directly from official party websites. The ordering of the parties and the information links were randomized in the Argentina, Canada 2017 and 2020, and US studies. In all instances, participants were able to explore as much information as they desired for as long as they wished. Figure 2.1 provides a screen capture of the information board used in the Canada 2017 study as an example.

Participants in the treatment conditions saw polling results displayed immediately above the information board. In Figure 2.2, we show an example of a treatment graph from the Canada 2017 study.[21] For five of the studies, the treatments provided information only on the actual level of public support for each of the four leading parties or alliances based on the polls at the time of the study (Argentina, Canada 2017 and 2020, and both US studies). In the Canada 2020 study, there were two possible treatment groups: one that presented the actual level of public support in graph format (similar to the treatments in the Argentina, Canada 2017, and two American studies) and another that presented the same information as text.[22] For four of the

I✦ Liberals	✿ Greens	𝒞 Conservatives	✦NDP NDP
Party: Statement... view	Party: Statement... view	Party: Statement... view	Party: Statement... view
Leader: Photo... view	Leader: Photo... view	Leader: Photo... view	Leader: Photo... view
Policy: Environment... view	Policy: Environment... view	Policy: Environment... view	Policy: Environment... view
Leader: Bio... view	Leader: Bio... view	Leader: Bio... view	Leader: Bio... view
Party: Endorsement... view	Party: Endorsement... view	Party: Endorsement ... view	Party: Endorsement... view
Policy: Economy.... view	Policy: Economy.... view	Policy: Economy.... view	Policy: Economy.... view

Figure 2.1: Sample Information Board (Canada 2017)

Note: Pictured is a sample of the information board presented to participants in the Canada 2017 study. The left-to-right ordering of the parties and the top-to-bottom ordering of the information links were both randomized by participant in the studies conducted in 2017 and later.

---

[21] The treatment and, where applicable, the turnout graph or text for each study are available in Online Appendix 2.3. A manipulation check to probe the efficacy of the treatments suggests a high level of uptake (see footnote 27).

[22] The text stated: "Liberals lead in National polls. A recent national poll finds that the Liberals would be the most popular choice if a federal election was held today. Of those surveyed, 39% indicated Liberal as their first choice, putting them 10 points ahead of the second place Conservatives, 23 points ahead of the NDP, and 32 points ahead of the Greens".

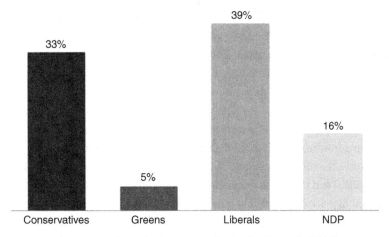

Figure 2.2: Sample Treatment Scenario (Canada 2017)
Note: Pictured is a sample polling treatment from the Canada 2017 study. For those in the treatment group, this image appeared directly above the information board shown in Figure 2.1.

studies, we manipulated poll results in two treatment groups: one that depicted the gap between the first- and second-place parties at approximately one quarter of the size of the actual gap (what we call "small gap"), and a second treatment that doubled the gap between the first- and second-place parties ("large gap") which existed in polls during fieldwork (Australia, Canada 2016, England, and New Zealand).

The Canada 2014 study consisted of eight treatments: four that included real party labels (like all other studies), and another four that used the exact same information but with fictional party labels (the parties were labeled Party Q, Party R, Party S, and Party T). After testing our hypotheses, we use this unique design element to explore whether our findings are driven by the use of genuine party labels. The Canada 2014 study was also unique in that it presented polling results in a cross-time line graph across fourteen polls depicting four hypothetical scenarios: a close race with the same party leading throughout, a close race with a change in the lead at the halfway point, a runaway race with the same party leading in all polls, and a runaway race with a change in the lead at about the mid-point. Because we found that impact of treatment was not conditional on whether the race was portrayed as static or dynamic, we have combined those treatment groups in the analyses that follow. We only maintain the distinction between close and runaway races.

Finally, it is important to note that we intentionally omitted any indication of poll source. We did this in an effort to ensure that source effects do not influence our results (see, e.g., Hovland and Weiss 1951; Petty and Wegener 1998; Miller and Krosnick 2000; Druckman 2001; Pornpitakpan 2004; Ismagilova et al. 2020). Given this design choice, we are confident that any poll effects we observe are a product of exposure to the polls, not the source of the polling information.

All studies prior to 2017 presented participants in the control group with the exact same information board as the treatment groups, except there was no poll graph above the information links. For the control group in the studies that took place in 2017 and beyond, a graph reporting turnout rates in recent elections was presented in place of the polling information. In the Canada 2020 study, we also included a second control group in which the turnout rates were reported in text format. Figure 2.3 shows an example of the control group in Canada 2017, and Table 2.1 provides a summary of the design elements for each study.

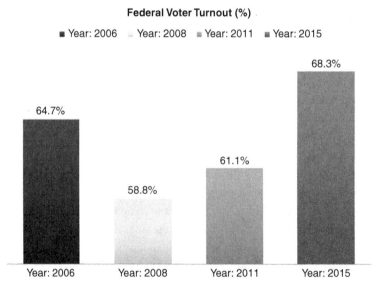

Figure 2.3: Sample Control Scenario for Post-2016 Studies (Canada 2017) **Note:** Pictured is a sample graph for a control condition from the Canada 2017 study. For those in the control group, this image appeared directly above the information board shown in Figure 2.1.

Table 2.1: Summary of Study Design Elements

	Number of Treatments	Issue info.	Party and Leader info.	Party and Links Order Random.	Large and Small Poll Gaps	Actual Poll Gap	Line Graph for Polls	Bar Graph for Polls	Text for Polls	Real Party Labels	Fictional Party Labels	Turnout Graph for Control	Turnout Text for Control
Canada 2014	8*	✓	-	-	✓	-	✓	-	-	✓	✓	-	-
Australia 2016	2	✓	-	-	✓	-	✓	-	-	✓	-	-	-
Canada 2016	2	✓	-	-	✓	-	-	✓	-	✓	-	-	-
England 2016	2		-	-	✓	-	-	✓	-	✓	-	-	-
New Zealand 2016	2		-	-	✓	-	-	✓	-	✓	-	-	-
Canada 2017	1	✓	✓	✓	-	✓	-	✓	-	✓	-	✓	-
Argentina 2018	1	✓	✓	✓	-	✓	-	✓	-	✓	-	✓	-
United States May 2018	1	✓	✓	✓	-	✓	-	✓	-	✓	-	✓	-
United States Nov. 2018	1	✓	✓	✓	-	✓	-	✓	-	✓	-	✓	-
Canada 2020	2	✓	✓	✓	-	✓	-	✓	✓	✓	-	✓	✓

Note: We reduce this to four groups in the empirical analyses.

* *Note:* We reduce this to four groups in the empirical analyses.

Unbeknownst to the participants, we recorded each piece of information that they accessed prior to voting and the amount of time they spent reviewing it. This allows us to measure the decision process that participants undertook. Upon completion of their information search, participants advanced to the vote screen where they cast their ballot. In all but the Canada 2014 study, participants had the option to choose "other" or "none" instead of voting for one of the four parties for which information was available.

After the removal of participants who did not advance beyond the pre-experiment survey and those who did not register a final vote preference, our sample size for each study ranges from approximately 2,000 to 2,700 respondents.[23] The sole exception is the Canada 2014 study, which had 1,525 participants. Table 2.2 offers a summary of the number of cases in each treatment group and the control group by study.

We subscribe to the arguments put forth by Mutz and Pemantle (2015: 205), who contend that "[r]andom assignment was either done correctly or it was not; there is no middle ground." Still, we include evidence of the success of the randomization process for those who may be skeptical. To do so, we use multinomial logistic regression to predict one's assignment to treatment as a function of several variables measured in the pre-experiment survey: partisanship, political ideology, political sophistication, satisfaction with democracy, gender, age, education, income, whether or not the respondent correctly answered a careless response question, and whether or not the respondent correctly identified the party or alliance leading in the national polls at the time of the study.[24] We could not reject the null hypothesis that each variable's effect was jointly zero in all studies.[25] Given that these observables are balanced across control and treatment groups, we are confident that any observed differences in our outcome variables across the treatment and control groups are

---

[23] Our Canada 2020 sample is reduced to 1,662 respondents for models with the count of information links accessed as the dependent variable. This is due to a technical error that prevents us from identifying whether 413 respondents clicked on the poll/turnout graphs or text to enlarge them as part of their information search (see Section 2.2.1).

[24] Gender, age, education, and income were measured following treatment in all studies conducted in 2017 and later. A careless response question and knowledge of actual poll standings was not asked in the Canada 2014 study. We did not ask about partisanship in the Argentina study.

[25] The p-values associated with the $\chi2$ tests of the joint significance of all coefficients are 0.28 (Canada 2014), 0.92 (Australia), 0.18 (Canada 2016), 0.45 (England), 0.26 (New Zealand), 0.55 (Argentina), 0.31 (Canada 2017), 0.17 (United States May 2018), 0.53 (United States November 2018), and 0.65 (Canada 2020). In total, we find 17 coefficients on specific variables that had a p-value smaller than 0.10, two-sided (see Online Appendix 2.4). These results—significance on 17 of 246 coefficients at the ten percent level—could have easily come about by chance. While we are not concerned with correcting for covariate imbalance, as discussed in the main text, we do control for socio-demographic characteristics in our analyses to increase precision.

Table 2.2: Group Sample Size by Study

	Actual Poll Gap – Graph	Actual Poll Gap – Text	Large Poll Gap	Small Poll Gap	Fake Labels - Large Gap	Fake Labels - Small Gap	Control - No Graph	Control - Graph	Control - Text	Total
Canada 2014	-	-	312	324	295	277	317*	-	-	1525
Australia 2016	-	-	745	753	-	-	722	-	-	2220
Canada 2016	-	-	787	731	-	-	720	-	-	2238
England 2016	-	-	778	758	-	-	701	-	-	2237
New Zealand 2016	-	-	696	711	-	-	749	-	-	2156
Canada 2017	1364	-	-	-	-	-	-	1361	-	2725
Argentina 2018	1268	-	-	-	-	-	-	1295	-	2563
United States May 2018	1286	-	-	-	-	-	-	1304	-	2590
United States Nov. 2018	1319	-	-	-	-	-	-	1242	-	2561
Canada 2020	531	505	-	-	-	-	-	503	536	2075

* *Note:* The control condition for Canada 2014 consists of two separate groups: one with real party labels (n=177) and one with fictional party labels (n=140).

a function of the treatments themselves and not systematic differences in the characteristics of participants in each group.[26]

2.2. Models and Measurement

To test our hypotheses, we use linear regression to estimate average treatment effects (ATEs), modeling the outcome variables as a function of randomly assigned treatment.[27] To increase precision, we control for socio-demographic characteristics: gender, age, education, and income. For all hypotheses, we report the results by study, along with a pooled model that combines all studies. In the pooled models, we include study-level fixed effects. In the following sub-sections, we outline our models and measurement choices sorted by our dependent concepts: information search and vote choice.

2.2.1. Information Search

Our primary measure of the information search is a count of the number of information links an individual viewed before casting a ballot.[28] As a robustness check, we run an additional set of models using a second outcome variable to capture this concept: the time in minutes that the respondents spent viewing information.[29] Table 2.3 reports the means and standard deviations for the two information search variables and the socio-demographic variables in every study.

---

[26] Random assignment to the control and treatment groups also alleviates any concern that knowledge of actual poll standings influences estimated treatment effects.

[27] Since not all of the treated respondents necessarily engaged with treatment, we are technically measuring the average treatment effect of assigning treatment, or the intention to treat (ITT) effect. With the exception of the Canada 2020 study, we did not include a manipulation check post-experiment to confirm that exposure to the stimulus was effective. But, given that participants had to scroll past the poll results displayed prominently at the top of the information board to access both the information links and the button to advance to the vote screen, we are confident that individuals would have at the very least viewed the information if not retained it. We expect that this is much like what takes place in a real-world scenario where voters are exposed to numerous bits of information that they may or may not consciously retain. Thus, we are comfortable interpreting our estimates of treatment effects as ATEs. Drawing from the Canada 2020 study, we find further support that our treatment was effective. In that study, we asked respondents which party was leading in the polls in both the pre- and post-experiment surveys. We observe an improvement in correct answers of approximately 16 percentage points for those exposed to the graph poll treatment and of 33 points for those exposed to the text poll treatment. For those in the control groups, mean knowledge of the leading party is virtually unchanged across the pre- and post-experiment surveys.

[28] This count excludes clicking on the treatment or control image to view in full screen.

[29] The method used to capture the time variable was updated for the Canada 2017 study and all subsequent studies. As such, direct comparison across studies conducted before and after 2017 is not possible. However, since all estimates are based on within-study comparison of ATEs, we draw upon this metric as a secondary indicator of the effort allotted to the information search.

Table 2.3: Summary Statistics

	Links viewed	Time viewing links	Lead party vote share	Age	Gender	Education	Income	Non-partisan	Political soph.	Confid. in polls
Canada 2014	4.96 (7.26)	2.97 (5.32)	0.30 (0.46)	46.81 (16.45)	0.49 (0.50)	1.93 (0.82)	1.94 (0.81)	0.40 (0.49)	0.03 (0.81)	-
Australia 2016	3.22 (5.67)	1.49 (2.41)	0.31 (0.47)	45.98 (15.58)	0.51 (0.50)	2.00 (0.95)	1.76 (0.75)	0.49 (0.50)	0.00 (0.86)	4.46 (2.53)
Canada 2016	2.81 (5.21)	1.61 (3.30)	0.46 (0.50)	45.20 (16.96)	0.51 (0.50)	2.05 (0.84)	2.01 (0.68)	0.41 (0.49)	-0.00 (0.84)	5.37 (2.43)
England 2016	2.37 (4.62)	1.41 (3.05)	0.32 (0.47)	49.30 (16.17)	0.51 (0.50)	1.84 (0.84)	2.12 (0.76)	0.47 (0.50)	-0.00 (0.85)	4.54 (2.55)
NZ 2016	3.31 (5.60)	1.87 (3.19)	0.37 (0.48)	46.49 (16.98)	0.51 (0.50)	1.89 (0.97)	2.06 (0.71)	0.47 (0.50)	0.01 (0.85)	5.08 (2.40)
Canada 2017	3.96 (6.56)	1.78 (3.28)	0.36 (0.48)	47.10 (16.78)	0.50 (0.50)	2.11 (0.83)	1.98 (0.79)	0.45 (0.50)	0.01 (0.83)	-
Argentina 2018	2.37 (4.47)	1.28 (2.58)	0.49 (0.50)	40.69 (14.23)	0.51 (0.50)	1.78 (0.95)	1.90 (0.84)	-	0.01 (0.82)	-
US May 2018	2.00 (4.65)	1.14 (2.75)	0.43 (0.50)	40.00 (13.91)	0.51 (0.50)	1.97 (0.91)	1.86 (0.80)	0.42 (0.49)	0.01 (0.84)	-
US Nov. 2018	1.92 (4.44)	1.04 (2.34)	0.45 (0.50)	42.73 (14.08)	0.55 (0.50)	2.04 (0.90)	1.88 (0.81)	0.35 (0.48)	0.01 (0.84)	-
Canada 2020	3.48 (6.02)	1.69 (3.25)	0.37 (0.48)	48.41 (17.92)	0.52 (0.50)	2.16 (0.86)	2.10 (0.81)	0.39 (0.49)	0.01 (0.84)	-

Note: Cells report the mean values with standard deviations in parentheses. Links is a raw count of the number of links viewed, time is expressed in minutes, lead party vote share is the proportion of the vote for the party depicted as leading in the polls, age is measured in years, gender is a dichotomous variable with man = 0 and woman = 1, education is measured on a four-point scale ranging from has not completed high school (= 0) to university degree (= 3), income is measured in terciles (1–3), non-partisan is a dichotomous variable with partisan = 0 and non-partisan = 1, political sophistication is a standardized index combining political knowledge and interest, and confidence in polls is a measure of how much confidence individuals have in the accuracy of poll results on a 0–10 scale (0 = no confidence).

Our first set of models assesses the overall impact that poll exposure has on the information search within each study and among all studies pooled together. They allow us to test our first hypothesis (H1a) on both measures of information seeking (number of links and number of minutes). We anticipate a decline in information gathering when polls are available.

To examine the potential heterogeneous impact of poll exposure according to a party's standings in the polls, our second set of models considers differences in the amount of information individuals explore by party. We analyse parties separately based on their poll standings (first, second, third, or fourth place). We expect parties depicted as trailing in the polls to suffer particularly from a decline in information search when individuals are exposed to polls (H1b).

As we explain in Section 1, we believe the impact of polls on the information search will vary according to individual-level traits, specifically partisanship, political sophistication, and how much confidence an individual has in pre-election polls. For partisanship, we use a dichotomous measure that distinguishes very and fairly strong partisan identifiers from those who indicated that they do not feel close to, or have only weak attachments to, any party (see Blais et al. 2001, 2002; Gidengil et al. 2012). We are able to do so based on the responses to two questions in the pre-experiment survey: the first asks if the individual feels an attachment to any party and, if so, a follow-up question asks the respondent to indicate the strength of their attachment.[30] We expect poll effects will be stronger among non-partisans (H3a).

We use a combination of political interest and political knowledge to measure political sophistication, reflecting its common multidimensional conceptualization (Fiske, Kinder, and Larter 1983; Zaller 1990, 1992; Miller 2011). We gauged each participant's level of political interest and knowledge in the pre-experiment survey. Political interest is measured with a self-reported 0–10 scale. Political knowledge is the proportion of correct answers to a series of four factual questions about politics.[31] To create our political sophistication index, we standardize and then sum the two scales for each study independently. We expect poll effects will be more pronounced among the less sophisticated (H4a).

The last individual-level factor that we consider is confidence in polling information. We argue that individuals with higher levels of confidence in polls will be more likely to be influenced by exposure to polls (H5a). To test this hypothesis, we included a pre-experiment survey question in four studies that asked respondents how much confidence they have in election campaign polls on a scale from 0 to 10 (Australia, Canada 2016, England, and New

---

[30] These questions were not asked in the Argentina study.

[31] The Canada 2014 study contained five trivia-type questions about politics. The political knowledge questions used in each study are available in Online Appendix 2.1.

Zealand). To mask the underlying intent of the study, this item was part of a confidence battery along with big business, media, unions, the courts, and the national government.

Our final set of information search models assesses how poll effects may differ according to the content of polls and how it is presented. We vary two aspects: the size of the gap reported in polling results and if the poll standings are presented graphically or via text.

We use five studies to assess how the size of the gap reported in the polling results affects behaviour (Australia, Canada 2014 and 2016, England, and New Zealand). In each of these studies, participants were randomly assigned to treatment groups that varied the size of the lead displayed in the polls. One of the treatment groups provided participants with graphical polling results where the lead party is ahead by a small margin, one quarter of the actual gap between the first- and second-place parties within that country at the time of our study (small gap). A second treatment group is presented with poll results revealing a wide lead, approximately twice the actual poll gap between the first- and second-place parties (large gap). By comparing changes in the information search across treatment groups, we can isolate the impact of the size of the reported lead on information gathering. We expect that polls will have a bigger effect when the gap between the lead and second-place parties is larger (H6a).

We then investigate how differences in the delivery of polling information influence information seeking. Specifically, we test whether poll effects differ according to whether results are presented in graphical form or via text, under the expectation that polls will matter more when conveyed textually (H7a). Here we draw upon the Canada 2020 study that incorporated treatments identical in every aspect with the exception of the poll information delivery mode.

We also explore the impact of employing actual versus fictional party labels in our experimental framework. Some poll experiments use mock elections, fake parties, and induced preferences (e.g., Forsythe et al. 1993; Merolla 2009; Großer and Schram 2010; Sinclair and Plott 2012; Klor and Winter 2017; Agranov et al. 2018). Others rely on real elections, actual parties, and existing preferences (e.g., Ansolabehere and Iyengar 1994; Meffert and Gschwend 2011; van der Meer et al. 2016; Dahlberg et al. 2017; Freden 2017; Gerber et al. 2020). We believe that it should be relatively easy to detect poll effects in an artificial environment to which individuals have no personal connection. In contrast, polls should be less likely to alter behaviour when the experimental environment involves preferences that are meaningful, important, anchored by a lifetime of experiences, and sticky. Testing for differences in conditions where actual party labels are available compared to similar conditions where they are not allows us to assess how much of an impact this design element has on our results. We draw upon the Canada 2014 study for this check. In addition to the availability of poll results, this study also included treatments that manipulated whether or not real party labels were available (Conservative Party or Party Q, Green Party or Party R, Liberal Party or Party S, and New Democratic Party or Party T). Given that everything but the availability of true party names was held constant across treatment groups, we can isolate the impact of polls according to the availability of party cues.

2.2.2. Vote Choice

In all voting models but the party-specific models (see below), our dependent variable is a dichotomous measure of whether the respondent voted for the party leading in the polls, as opposed to voting for any other party or abstaining. We report the means and standard deviations of this variable by study in Table 2.3.

Our vote choice models follow the same order as our information search models. First, we estimate the overall impact of the poll treatments on vote choice within each study and among all studies combined, anticipating a bandwagon effect (H2a). Then, we consider the impact polls have on the vote for each political party according to the party's position in the polls (first, second, third, or fourth). We compare the vote share that a given party received in the control group against the share when the party's poll standing was reported to treated respondents, expecting some desertion of the trailing parties (H2b).

We next consider whether individual-level differences moderate the relationship between poll exposure and vote choice. We again consider partisanship, political sophistication, and confidence in the polls as potential moderators, expecting stronger polling effects among non- partisans (H3b), the less sophisticated (H4b), and those who trust polls (H5b).

Lastly, we ascertain how differences in the information conveyed by polls and the way in which this information is presented influence the size of poll effects on vote choice. As we explain above, we varied the size of the lead of the frontrunner over the second-place party and the delivery mode of the polling information (graphical versus text). We predict bandwagon voting will be more frequent when the race is not close (H6b) and when poll results are described with text rather than presented graphically (H7b). As we do in the analyses of participants' information searches, we conclude the analyses of vote choice by assessing the impact of using real versus fictional party labels in our experiment.

Table 2.4 presents a summary of all hypotheses with the corresponding studies that we draw upon to test them.

Table 2.4: Summary of Hypotheses

Hypotheses	Studies
H1a: Exposure to polls will reduce information seeking. H1b: Exposure to polls will reduce information seeking, especially for parties trailing in the polls.	All studies
H2a: Exposure to polls will increase the likelihood of voting for the lead party. H2b: Exposure to polls will decrease the likelihood of voting for parties trailing in the polls.	All studies
H3a: Exposure to polls will reduce information seeking, especially for non-partisans. H3b: Exposure to polls will increase the likelihood of voting for the lead party, especially for non-partisans.	All studies except Argentina
H4a: Exposure to polls will reduce information seeking, especially for those who are less politically sophisticated. H4b: Exposure to polls will increase the likelihood of voting for the lead party, especially for those who are less politically sophisticated.	All studies
H5a: Exposure to polls will reduce information seeking, especially for individuals with higher levels of confidence in polls. H5b: Exposure to polls will increase the likelihood of voting for the lead party, especially for individuals with higher levels of confidence in polls.	Australia 2016 Canada 2016 England 2016 New Zealand 2016
H6a: Exposure to polls will reduce information seeking, especially when the gap between the lead and second-place party is larger. H6b: Exposure to polls will increase the likelihood of voting for the lead party, especially when the gap between the lead and second-place party is larger.	Canada 2014 Australia 2016 Canada 2016 England 2016 New Zealand 2016
H7a: Exposure to polls will reduce information seeking, especially when polling results are conveyed by text. H7b: Exposure to polls will increase the likelihood of voting for the lead party, especially when polling results are conveyed by text.	Canada 2020

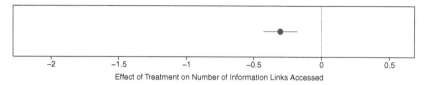

Figure 2.4: Sample Graphical Exhibit of Results

2.3. Presentation of Results

For all analyses, we present the ATEs graphically, with corresponding numerical estimates reported in the Online Appendix. Figure 2.4 shows a simplified example of our graphical exhibits.[32] The point estimate depicts the ATE of poll exposure on the number of information links accessed when all studies are pooled together. Here, we see that those who were exposed to polls accessed approximately 0.3 fewer information links than those in the control groups, who did not see polling results. The horizontal lines to each side of the point estimate represent the 90% confidence interval. When both lines fall to the left or to the right of zero, the result is statistically significant at a level of one minus the size of the confidence interval. Thus, in this example, the estimated ATE is statistically significant at the 0.10 level (two-sided), because the 90% confidence interval does not overlap zero.

We turn now to our first empirical section: an assessment of how public opinion polls influence the information search that individuals undertake prior to casting their ballot.

3. The Effects of Polls on the Search for Campaign Information

In this first results section, we put our experimental election platform to use, seeking to understand how exposure to polls influences the amount of information that participants gather while in our simulation. Following our hypotheses and analysis strategy (see Section 2), we initially test for unconditional effects of poll exposure. Subsequently, we assess whether individual-level factors, the content of the polls, and how the polls are presented condition the impact that viewing polls has on the information search.

3.1. Do Polls Lead Voters to Seek Less Information?

We begin with a model that compares information seeking between those who are exposed to polls and those who are not. Our guiding expectation, put forth in our first hypothesis (H1a), is that exposure to polls will reduce the amount of

---

[32] See Online Appendix 2.5 for full numerical results. All replication files and supplementary appendix material are available at: https://www.cambridge.org/RSF_Appendix.

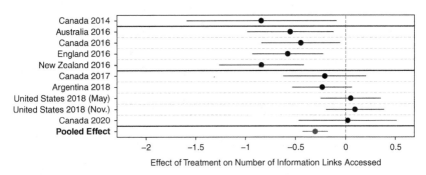

Figure 3.1: The Impact of Poll Exposure on the Number of Information Links Accessed

information gathered. In Figure 3.1, we display the average treatment effects (ATEs) of poll exposure on the number of information links accessed.[33] In Figure 3.2, we show the impact of our treatments on a second measure of the effort allotted to the information search: the time spent viewing information, measured in minutes. Recall that all estimates are from linear regression models of the outcome variables on treatment status and are adjusted for gender, age, education, and income.[34] In the pooled models that combine all studies, we also include study-level fixed effects.

As shown in Figure 3.1, the pooled effect of poll exposure is negative and statistically significant; individuals exposed to polls considered approximately one third of an information link fewer than those who did not see polls. When we examine the results by study, we find that in all but the two US studies and Canada 2020, the ATEs are in the expected direction (negative), and they are statistically distinguishable from zero in five of the ten studies.[35] On the whole, these results indicate that exposure to poll information tends to decrease the amount of information individuals accessed prior to lodging their voting preference. In substantive terms, the effects are small, but they are nontrivial. The mean number of links viewed in the control groups is about three, meaning the

---

[33] Full numerical results for all models are available in Online Appendix 3.1.

[34] When we estimate treatment effects on the time spent viewing information, we also include a control for whether or not respondents clicked to view the poll or past election turnout results in full screen. Recall from Section 2 that the control groups in our studies prior to 2017 did not have this option, as they did not see turnout graphs.

[35] While it may be tempting to try to infer meaning from the cross-time differences reported in Figure 3.1 (as well as from subsequent results reported below), we caution against doing so. Given the combination of country-level effects, changes to our experimental design, and election-specific factors within and across countries, it is not possible to credibly disentangle what may be driving any observed intertemporal differences in effects.

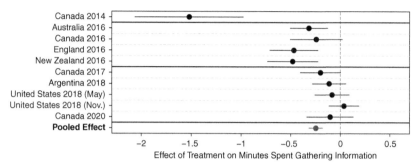

Figure 3.2: The Impact of Poll Exposure on the Amount of Time Spent Gathering Information

pooled effect of treatment is to reduce the average amount of links viewed by about one ninth.

The results pertaining to our second measure of information seeking, the time spent gathering information, are shown in Figure 3.2. In all but the second United States study, individuals exposed to poll information spent less time accessing information than those in the control condition. In four of the ten studies, and in the pooled model, the estimated treatment effect is meaningfully different from zero. The strongest result is observed in Canada 2014, where the treatment group spent about 90 fewer seconds searching information than those in the control group. Across all ten studies, treatment decreases the amount of time spent seeking information by about 15 seconds. To contextualize this effect, the mean time spent exploring information in the control groups is approximately 94 seconds. These results largely confirm the first set of findings; the amount of time spent gathering information is lower among those who are exposed to polls than among those in the control condition.[36]

3.2. Effects by Party

Next, we consider how the information conveyed in the polls may affect information gathering differently according to party popularity. Our expectation, as stated in hypothesis H1b, is that exposure to polls will reduce information seeking most notably for material pertaining to parties trailing in the polls. To assess whether treatment effects are conditional on parties' poll standings, we estimate the impact of treatment on the number of links accessed relating to

---

[36] In subsequent investigations of the impact of polls on the information search discussed in this section, we do not show graphs pertaining to the time spent seeking information. These robustness checks are presented in Online Appendix 3.2.

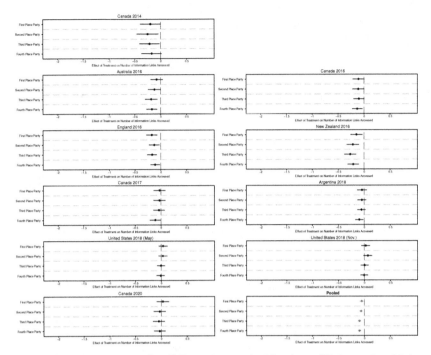

Figure 3.3: The Impact of Poll Exposure on the Number of Information Links Accessed, According to Party Standing

the first, second, third, and fourth place competitors separately. The results are presented in Figure 3.3.

There is some evidence to suggest that the attention allotted to trailing parties decreases the most when polls are shown. Five of the studies tend to fit this pattern (Argentina, Australia, and Canada 2016, 2017, and 2020). In the pooled model, the treatments significantly diminish exploration of every party's information links, but the ATEs are slightly larger in magnitude for parties in third and fourth place, and the differences between the ATEs for the third- and fourth-place parties and those of the first- and second-place parties are statistically significant (the two-sided p-values are less than 0.10 for each of the four comparisons). Overall, it appears that the small reduction in the information search resulting from poll exposure applies to all political parties, but somewhat more to those at the lower end of the poll standings.[37]

---

[37] We do not have a reliable measure for time spent viewing information by party. Therefore, we are unable to run additional analyses with time as the dependent variable for these models.

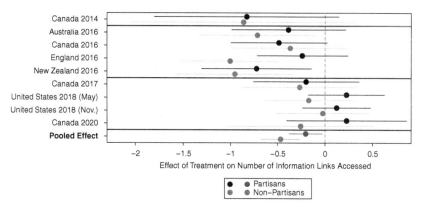

Figure 3.4: The Impact of Poll Exposure on the Number of Information Links Accessed, According to Party Identification

3.3. Individual-Level Conditioners: Party Identification, Political Sophistication, and Confidence in Polls

We next search for heterogeneity in the influence of polls within the electorate, assessing whether treatment effects vary according to partisanship, political sophistication and confidence in the accuracy of polls.[38] To do so, we interact treatment status with each conditioning variable, estimating separate models for all three. We begin with partisanship, and hypothesis H3a, which states that exposure to polls will reduce information seeking most notably for non-partisans. The results are reported in Figure 3.4.

The patterns are consistent with our hypothesis in most of the studies. Still, differences in ATEs across partisans and non-partisans tend to be small, and they are not discernible from zero at conventional significance levels except in the England study, in which the two-sided p-value associated with the difference in the ATEs is 0.07.[39] In the pooled model, the negative impact of poll exposure on the information search is significant among both groups, but is a bit stronger

---

[38] We proceed with recognition that the individual-level conditioning variables are observed rather than randomly manipulated. As such, they may be correlated with any number of relevant observed and unobserved factors. Thus, while we are able to identify the causal effect of treatment at different values of the conditioning variables, we cannot identify *why* treatment sizes may differ (Kam and Trussler 2017). That being the case, our controls for gender, age, education, and income, which we include to increase precision, as we discuss in Section 2, also help to lessen bias from confounding.

[39] We remind readers that overlap in two 90% confidence intervals does not necessarily indicate that the two associated point estimates are not significantly different from one another at the 10% level. Assuming equal sample sizes and standard errors, the confidence level required to use the "overlap test" to approximate whether two point estimates are statistically different at the 10% level would be about 76% (Julious 2004).

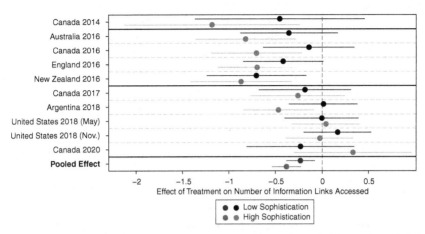

Figure 3.5: The Impact of Poll Exposure on the Number of Information Links Accessed, According to Political Sophistication

for non-partisans, with the difference in the ATEs just missing conventional levels of statistical significance (two-sided *p*-value = 0.11). When we estimate poll effects by partisanship with time spent seeking information as the dependent variable (results not shown; see Online Appendix 3.2), we find a similar pattern, albeit with some variation across countries and the pooled model yielding less decisive results than those reported in Figure 3.4. As such, there is some support for our expectation that poll exposure has a greater downward impact on non-partisans' information search, but it is weak. We revisit the implications of this in Section 4, in which we consider the impact of polls on voting behaviour for partisans and non-partisans.

Hypothesis H4a states that exposure to polls will reduce information seeking most sharply for those who are less politically sophisticated. We report the results of the test of this hypothesis in Figure 3.5, in which we show ATEs for those at the 25th and 75th percentiles of the sophistication measure, labeled "Low Sophistication" and "High Sophistication," respectively (see Section 2 for more details on our measure of political sophistication).

Not only do the results fail to support hypothesis H4a, they tend to contradict it. In all but the studies conducted in the United States in May 2018 and Canada in 2020, it is the highly sophisticated who are most likely to reduce their information search after poll exposure. But the differences between the two groups are small and only statistically significant in Argentina (the two-sided *p*-value associated with the difference in ATEs is 0.08). In the pooled model, the difference between the two ATEs is not distinguishable from zero (two-sided *p*-value = 0.17). Results from models with time spent seeking information as the dependent variable provide even less evidence of variation across sophistication groups (see Online Appendix 3.2), though high sophisticates are most apt to decrease the time they spend on their information search when exposed to polls in six studies and in the pooled model (but never significantly more so than low sophisticates).

Thus, contrary to what we expected, it appears that the more politically sophisticated segment of the electorate is slightly more inclined to draw upon the poll cue and to reduce the amount of information with which they engage and the time they spend engaging with information, but this finding is statistically uncertain. We revisit this in Section 4, where we examine the effects of poll exposure on vote choice according to the level of political sophistication.

Lastly among the individual-level conditioners, we turn to confidence in polls. Hypothesis H5a proposes that poll effects will be stronger for individuals who are more confident in the accuracy of polling information. Figure 3.6 displays the ATEs for those at the 25th and 75th percentiles of the poll confidence measure, labeled "Low Confidence in Polls" and "High Confidence in Polls," respectively.

Surprisingly, confidence in poll information is of limited consequence for the effect of poll exposure on the information search. In only one of the four studies for which this measure is available, that conducted in New Zealand, do we observe any sizable or significant difference in ATEs across low and high confidence groups (two-sided p-value = 0.07). In the other three studies, as well as the pooled model, confidence in the polls has virtually no impact on the influence of poll exposure on the information search. This indicates that, to the extent that polls shape information seeking, it does not matter whether or not the recipient of the polling information is confident in its veracity. This is also true when we use the time spent seeking information as the dependent variable (see Online Appendix 3.2).

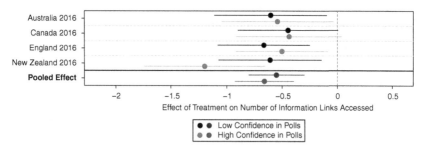

Figure 3.6: The Impact of Poll Exposure on the Number of Information Links Accessed, According to Confidence in Polls

3.4. The Influence of Poll Content and Presentation

In the next set of models, we examine how the content presented in polls affects the information search. We begin by considering the influence of the size of the lead depicted in polls. Hypothesis H6a asserts that exposure to polls will reduce information seeking most notably when the gap between the first- and second-place parties is larger. To test this, we draw upon the results of the Canada 2014 and 2016 studies, as well as those conducted in Australia, England, and New Zealand. As we discuss in Section 2, we included in these five studies treatments that presented poll content showing a "large gap" between the frontrunner and runner-up (approximately twice the gap reported in the national polls within the country at the time of the experiment) and treatments that presented a "small gap" (approximately a quarter of the gap reported in the polls). Figure 3.7 illustrates the results.

In only two of the five studies, Australia and New Zealand, do we find results in the expected direction, although the difference between ATEs in both studies is negligible and not statistically significant. The pooled model shows that the ATEs are almost identical for the small and large gap conditions, a finding that is replicated with time spent seeking information as the outcome variable (see Online Appendix 3.2). Put simply, our results indicate that the size of the lead portrayed in the polls makes little difference in the information search; individuals exposed to election polls reduce their information gathering equally regardless of whether the leading party is ahead by a large or small margin.

Our next investigation assesses whether the way in which the polling results are presented impacts the information search. To do so, we draw upon the Canada 2020 study, in which participants were randomly assigned to poll treatments that conveyed the same information graphically (similar to the treatments in the other studies) or in text format. We estimate the ATEs by

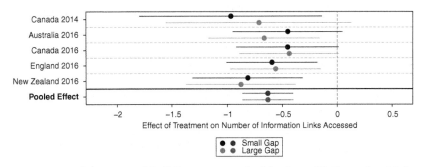

Figure 3.7: The Impact of Poll Exposure on the Number of Information Links Accessed, According to the Size of the Lead

comparing individuals within each of the treatment groups to those in the corresponding control group (election turnout presented in a graph or as text, respectively). Our expectation is that exposure to polls will do more to reduce information seeking when polling results are communicated by text (H7a). Findings are presented in Figure 3.8.

The results show that the text treatment does reduce the information search to a greater extent than the graph treatment. However, in neither treatment group do we find the difference between treatment and control to reach traditional levels of statistical significance. Furthermore, the difference in the treatment effects is not itself statistically distinguishable from zero at any conventional level. This is true regardless of whether we examine the number of links accessed or the time spent exploring information (see Online Appendix 3.2). Contrary to hypothesis H7a, the way in which the polling information is presented does not alter the impact of poll exposure on the information search.

Might our weak results reflect our effort to increase external validity by including actual party labels in our design? As we note above, one possible explanation for stronger experimental evidence of poll effects relative to obser-vational studies may be the artificial environment of the experimental work. To test this possibility, and to gauge the role of pre-existing orientations towards the various political parties, we examine the impact of removing the names of political parties from the poll standings and replacing them with generic markers (e.g., "Party Q"). Here we rely on the Canada 2014 study, in which we included poll treatments with and without actual party labels. The results from the associated model are presented in Figure 3.9.

While participants did explore fewer links, relative to the control group, when exposed to poll results devoid of party labels than when exposed to polls that identify the parties, the difference between the two ATEs is small and fails to meet conventional levels of statistical significance. The ATEs themselves are just shy of significance. In the model with time spent seeking information as the

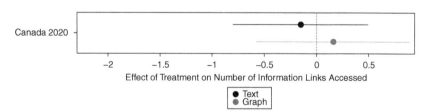

Figure 3.8: The Impact of Poll Exposure on the Number of Information Links Accessed, According to the Mode of Presentation of Polling Results

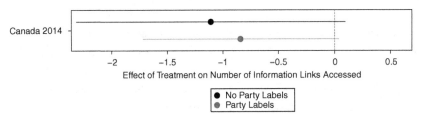

Figure 3.9: The Impact of Poll Exposure on the Number of Information Links Accessed, According to Whether or Not Parties Were Named

dependent variable, the treatment effects are practically identical with and without the inclusion of real party labels, although in both groups the ATEs are found to be statistically significant (two-sided p-value < 0.10; see Online Appendix 3.2). So, even when individuals are presented with a polling scenario lacking meaningful context (i.e., party names), they are hardly more inclined to draw upon poll cues. Exposure to polls reduces the information search whether or not voters are cognisant of the actual parties in contention.

3.5. Summary

Our results show that, on average, individuals exposed to polling results reduce the effort they allot to their decision-making process. Those who see polls access slightly less information and spend slightly less time seeking information about the competing parties. Contrary to expectations, we find limited evidence that individual- and poll-level factors condition the impact of viewing election polls on the information search that citizens undertake prior to voting. That is, we do not find much support for the notion that the effects of our polling treatments are heterogeneous; polls reduced the information search, regardless of individual- and poll-level differences.

In the next section, we consider how poll exposure affects voting behaviour. Specifically, we determine whether seeing polls shapes a voter's propensity to "jump on the bandwagon" and cast a ballot for the party shown to be leading in the polls.

4. The Effects of Polls on Vote Choice

As we discuss in Section 3, poll exposure somewhat reduces the amount of effort voters put into learning about the competitors in an election. For the most part, this negative effect persists across different types of individuals and regardless of the polls' content and how the polling information is presented. We now consider the impact poll exposure has on vote choice. As we outline in the first section, the primary focus of research on the consequences of polls has been their relevance for vote choice, and the dominant argument contends that poll exposure produces a bandwagon effect, prompting voters to choose the candidate leading in the polls. However, extant empirical evidence offers mixed support for the bandwagon thesis (see Section 1). In this section, we build upon the existing literature, drawing from our cross-national experiments to directly assess the influence poll exposure exerts on vote choice. Similar to the approach employed in the preceding section, we first test for unconditional effects, and we subsequently examine whether individual- and poll-level factors condition the impact of polls on the votes people cast.

4.1. A Test of the Bandwagon Effect

Hypothesis H2a, based on the bandwagon claim, asserts that exposure to polls will increase the likelihood that one votes for the party depicted as leading. To evaluate this, we create an outcome variable that differentiates those who voted for the lead party from those who voted for any other party. (Recall from Section 2 that we asked participants in our election simulations to cast a vote for one of the competing parties after exiting the information board.) For this test and all subsequent analyses in this section, we use linear regression to model the outcome variable as a function of assignment to the polling treatment, adjusting for gender, age, education, and income. In the pooled models that combine all studies, we also include study-level fixed effects. We report average treatment effects (ATEs) of poll exposure on the probability of bandwagon voting in Figure 4.1.[40]

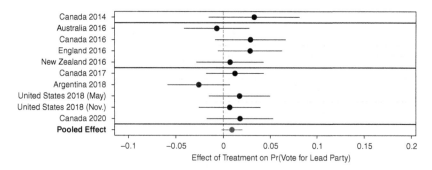

Figure 4.1: The Impact of Poll Exposure on Vote for the Lead Party

---

[40] Full numerical results for all models are available in Online Appendix 4.1.

Our results provide only limited support for the bandwagon effect. While the ATE of exposure to polls is positive in eight of the ten studies, as well as in the pooled model, the magnitude of the impact is marginal, and in no instance does the ATE achieve conventional levels of statistical significance (the two-sided *p*-value associated with the ATE in the pooled model is 0.17). As such, we cannot conclude that, overall, exposure to polls increases individuals' propensity to vote for the lead party.

4.2. Effects by Party

While we find little evidence that poll exposure shapes the vote share of the party shown to be ahead in the polls, it may be the case that polls affect support for trailing parties. Hypothesis H2b puts forth the expectation that voters who see polls will be less likely to vote for parties depicted as trailing than those who do not. To test this, we estimate the impact of treatment on the probability of voting for each party by poll standing. The resultant ATEs are presented in Figure 4.2.

We uncover negligible support for hypothesis H2b. Looking at the pooled results, the probability of voting for the third- and fourth-place parties decreases when respondents are shown polls, consistent with strategic desertion. However, only the ATE related to the third-place party is statistically distinguishable from zero, and the size of the effect is small. The probability of voting for the third-place party in the control groups is about 0.13: viewing the polls decreases this by about one percentage point.

Regarding the second-place party, there is borderline evidence of an underdog effect. In four of the ten studies (Argentina, Australia, Canada 2017, and New Zealand), the second-place party receives a poll-related boost in support greater than that observed for the lead party. This is also manifest in the pooled results, in which the ATE of poll exposure on voting for the runner-up is positive, small (about one percentage point), statistically significant, and slightly larger than the effect of poll exposure on frontrunner voting (though the difference in the two ATEs is not statistically significant by any conventional standard, with an associated two-sided *p*-value of 0.89).

4.3. Individual-Level Conditioners: Party Identification, Political Sophistication, and Confidence in Polls

We next consider how poll effects on vote choice may vary according to individual-level characteristics. To test for conditional effects, we interact treatment with each conditioning variable, using separate models for each. We begin with partisanship. In Section 3, we find that poll exposure has a stronger

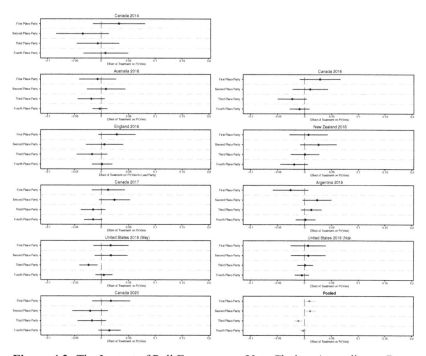

Figure 4.2: The Impact of Poll Exposure on Vote Choice, According to Party Standing

negative impact on the amount of information sought among non- partisans than among partisans (though the difference in the effect sizes just misses traditional levels of statistical significance). Since non-partisans may access less information than partisans when exposed to polls, they may also be more likely to simply plump for the frontrunner. This comports with the expectations of hypothesis H3b, which states that exposure to polls will increase the likelihood of voting for the lead party most dramatically for non-partisans. Figure 4.3 presents the results relevant for this prediction.

In line with expectations, in all studies but Canada 2016 and 2020, non-partisans exposed to polls are indeed more likely to vote for the frontrunner than partisans given the same stimulus. In other words, the ATEs of poll exposure are often bigger for non-partisans. In the pooled model, the ATE for non-partisans is about four percentage points, whereas for partisans it is essentially zero. And the difference between these two ATEs is itself statistically significant (two-sided p-value = 0.01). These results also offer some insight into the findings reported in Figure 4.1: poll exposure does raise support slightly for the lead party, but only within a subset of the population, namely those without partisan attachments. We return to the potential implications of this finding in the conclusion.

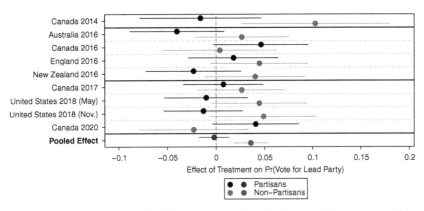

Figure 4.3: The Impact of Poll Exposure on Vote for the Lead Party, According to Party Identification

In Section 3, we do not find that less sophisticated electors are most likely to reduce the amount of campaign information they access when polls are available. Though differences are trivial, disengagement with party information is, if anything, greater among the more sophisticated when exposed to polling results. Does this mean that political sophisticates are more likely to jump on the bandwagon when they see polls? Such a pattern would yield evidence counter to hypothesis H4b, in which we posit that exposure to polls will increase the likelihood of voting for the lead party most notably among the less politically sophisticated. Results of our test of this hypothesis are presented in Figure 4.4. In the figure, we show ATEs for individuals at the 25th and 75th percentiles of our sophistication index, labeled "Low Sophistication" and "High Sophistication," respectively.

Only one of the ten studies, Canada 2017, exhibits sophistication-conditional treatment effects. In that experiment, the ATE among those who lack sophistication is larger than that of their more sophisticated counterparts, consistent with hypothesis H4b (the two-sided p-value associated with the difference in the ATEs is 0.02). In the other studies, the ATEs, as well as the differences between them, tend to be very small and imprecisely estimated. And, in the pooled model, there is no indication that either less or more sophisticated participants become more likely to vote for the leading party when exposed to polls. Our results provide very little evidence that political sophistication alters the impact of polls on bandwagon voting.

Next, we consider the conditioning impact of the amount of confidence individuals have in the campaign polls themselves. As proposed in hypothesis H5b, we expect that those with a greater level of confidence in poll

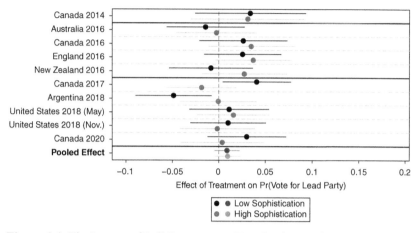

Figure 4.4: The Impact of Poll Exposure on Vote for the Lead Party, According to Political Sophistication

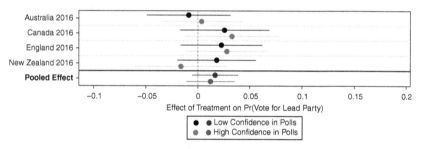

Figure 4.5: The Impact of Poll Exposure on Vote for the Lead Party, According to Confidence in Polls

results are more likely to be influenced by exposure to them. Figure 4.5 displays the ATEs for those at the 25th and 75th percentiles of the poll confidence measure, labeled "Low Confidence in Polls" and "High Confidence in Polls," respectively.

Contrary to our expectations, but similar to the results shown in Section 3 with regard to campaign information seeking, a respondent's level of confidence in polling results has little impact on her likelihood of changing voting behaviour as a result of seeing polls. None of the studies nor the pooled model reveal evidence that people with any degree of confidence in polls are more likely to vote for the frontrunner when confronted with polling results. Again, like in the previous section, it does not seem to matter whether or not the person exposed to polls trusts the information being presented.

4.4. The Influence of Poll Content and Presentation

Our final set of models investigates whether the content and presentation mode of polls moderates the impact that they have on vote choices. We begin by examining the influence of the size of the lead of the first-place party over its closest contender on the effect of polls on bandwagon voting. Hypothesis H6b states that exposure to polls will increase the likelihood of voting for the leading party more notably when the gap between the first- and second-place parties is larger. Five studies offer pertinent data: Australia, Canada 2014 and 2016, England, and New Zealand. As we discuss in Section 2, each of these studies contained treatments that presented polling information signalling a "large gap" between the top two parties (approximately twice the actual gap in the national polls within the country at the time of the experiment), and treatments that signalled a "small gap" (approximately a quarter of the gap in the polls at the time). Results are illustrated in Figure 4.6.

While the results are generally in line with expectations, in only one case, New Zealand, do we find a notable difference in ATEs according to gap size (two-sided p-value = 0.04), though neither individual ATE is itself statistically distinguishable from zero. In the pooled model, there is a significant impact of poll exposure on the probability of voting for the lead party when gap size is large, while the impact is essentially nil when gap size is small. However, the difference between these two ATEs does not achieve conventional levels of statistical significance (two-sided p-value = 0.13). Thus, there is limited substantiation that poll exposure has a bigger effect on frontrunner voting when that party is far ahead in the polls.

Our final hypothesis examines the link between the mode of poll delivery and the effect of poll exposure on the vote (H7b). We expect that seeing polls will increase the likelihood of voting for the frontrunner more notably when polling information is conveyed by text. Results of our test of this hypothesis are presented in Figure 4.7.

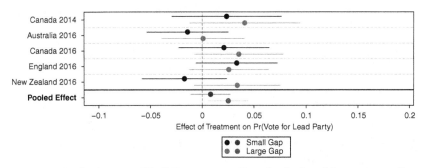

Figure 4.6: The Impact of Poll Exposure on Vote for the Lead Party, According to the Size of the Lead

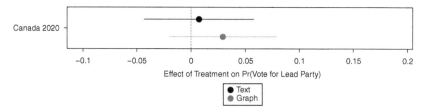

Figure 4.7: The Impact of Poll Exposure on Vote for the Lead Party, According to the Mode of Presentation of Polling Results

The results offer no support for hypothesis H7b. Providing poll information in text format does not produce a stronger bandwagon effect compared to when the same information is presented via a chart. If anything, the results indicate a greater impact of polls in the case of the graph treatment. However, neither the individual ATEs nor the difference in ATEs across treatments is statistically different from zero. It seems that the way the polling information is delivered does little to alter the overall impact of poll exposure on the likelihood of voting for the leading party.

Might the limited poll effects observed here reflect our use of actual party labels in our studies? The short answer is no. We tested this in the Canada 2014 study, which included poll treatments with and without real party labels. Figure 4.8 displays the results of this analysis. As the results show, regardless of whether or not real party labels are visible, exposure to polls does not have a significant impact on the probability of voting for the frontrunner. Moreover, the ATEs of the no-label and with-label polling scenarios are essentially equal.

4.5. Summary

We began this section with a simple question: Do public opinion polls affect voting behaviour? The results from our collection of studies from several countries suggest that their impact is limited. There are some indications that viewing polling results decreases support for trailing parties and increases support for the second-place party. Regarding the bandwagon effect, while partisan identifiers are unaffected by polls, we find that those without a partisan attachment are more likely to vote for the party depicted as leading in the polls. We also uncover some evidence that polls can generate bandwagon behaviour when the portrayed gap in public support between the frontrunner and the runner-up is particularly large. In the following, concluding section, we reflect on the implications of our empirical findings for the academic literature and for electoral management.

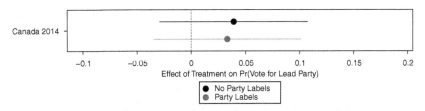

Figure 4.8: The Impact of Poll Exposure on Vote for the Lead Party, According to Whether or Not Parties Were Named

5. Conclusion

This work stems from a seemingly simple question: do public opinion polls influence individuals' political behaviour and preferences? Guided by this question, we began this project recognizing that observational studies are limited in their ability to credibly identify poll effects. We also felt that, in order to assess the impact of polls on information seeking, we needed a way to directly measure engagement with political material. We thus built an experimental online election platform that allowed us to randomly manipulate exposure to polls and also to track participants' activity in a simulated election environment.

We ultimately conducted ten experiments across six countries on four continents: Argentina, Australia, Canada, New Zealand, the United Kingdom (England only), and the United States. In the end, we find only limited evidence that exposure to polls affects political information searches and voting behaviour. Our results show that polls' effects are small. Still, we are not discouraged by these minute and sometimes null findings. In fact, we believe they have important implications for both public policy and academic research. In this section, we discuss these implications of our work. First, though, we summarize our empirical findings and reflect on potential criticisms of our research design.

5.1. Review of Our Findings

Our empirical analyses are presented in Sections 3 and 4. In Section 3, we probe whether exposure to polling results affects how much information people access when deciding how to vote and the amount of time they spend doing so. In Section 4, we examine the impact of poll exposure on vote choice.

Our first test in Section 3 concerns our expectation that seeing polls reduces the amount of information gathered during an election campaign (H1a). We find support for this, though the substantive effect of polls on the information search is not large. Also, we unearth evidence that reductions in information seeking are slightly more pronounced for parties trailing in the polls (H1b). Taken together, these results suggest that polls can lead to lower attention to campaign information.

We then assess whether the impact of polls on information seeking varies across individuals according to partisan attachment (H3a), political sophistication (H4a), and confidence in the polls (H5a). We find limited support that the influence of polls is stronger among non-partisans, but, counter to our expectations, we uncover no indication that it is conditioned by sophistication or perceived poll credibility. This latter finding is both surprising and important, as it demonstrates that polls matter for the information search even for people who claim they do not trust them. However, we note the possibility that the omission of a poll source in our studies could have played a part in this null finding. It may be that it is not so much that individuals do not trust *all* polls, but rather they take exception with certain poll sources (e.g., survey houses or media outlets). A possible avenue for future research is to better address how poll effects may differ across individuals with a general mistrust in polls compared to those with source-specific scepticism.

Next, we investigate whether the negative impact of polls on information seeking is greatest when the race is less competitive (H6a) and when polling results are conveyed by text rather than graphics (H7a). Neither of these expectations are corroborated; runaway races do not strengthen the effect of polls on the information search, and presenting polling data with a clear, text-based statement about a first-place party's commanding lead does not increase its efficacy.

Turning to the examinations of Section 4, we first assess whether exposure to polls increases the likelihood of voting for the leading party (H2a). The effect of polls on bandwagon voting is positive but small and estimated without much credibility. We also gauge whether exposure to polls decreases the likelihood of voting for trailing parties (H2b), finding some evidence that voters strategically defect from the third-place party. Additionally, we observe some traces of an underdog effect, whereby the second-place party benefits from desertion of parties with no chance of winning.

We then ascertain whether the impact of polls on vote choice is moderated by partisanship (H3b), political sophistication (H4b), and confidence in the polls (H5b). The bandwagon effect is concentrated among non-partisans, who are less likely to have sticky preferences. This may, in part, offer some reconciliation for studies with conflicting findings about the bandwagon thesis: it would seem that polls can induce bandwagon behaviour, but the effects are largely limited to those without a partisan attachment. However, as with the information search, political sophistication and perceived poll credibility do not condition the impact of polls on vote choice.

Next, we test whether the influence of polls on voting behaviour is most notable when the race is not close (H6b) and when polling results are communicated by words rather than a chart (H7b). Poll exposure has a stronger (though still small) effect on frontrunner voting when that party enjoys a wide lead over the runner-up. This suggests that polls are most likely to engender a bandwagon effect when it is clear that a lot of people have already jumped on the bandwagon. Once again analogous to what we observe for the information search, we find no evidence that the mode of presentation, textual versus graphical, moderates the impact of polls on vote choice.

5.2. Did We Underestimate Poll Effects?

A sceptical reader might assume that we have underestimated the true efficacy of public opinion polls. First, one might worry that our treatments went unnoticed by a large portion of participants. As we note in Section 2, not all of the treated respondents necessarily engaged with the treatments. Thus, in our analyses, we calculated the average treatment effect (ATE) of assigning treatment, or the intention to treat (ITT) effect. We interpret the ITTs as ATEs due to our belief that our election simulations mimic the real-world environment in which voters are exposed to numerous bits of information that they may or may not consciously retain. Still, if a large number of participants simply ignored the treatment or were otherwise fully unmanipulated, these ITT effects would be considerably smaller than true treatment effects, meaning citizens would be more likely to be influenced by exposure to polls in reality.

To probe the efficacy of treatments within our platform, we included manipulation checks in the last study we conducted, which was fielded in Canada in 2020. We found substantively and statistically significant improvements in the accurate identification of the leading party among individuals who were exposed to polls. In footnote 27 of Section 2, we report that those shown a graphical depiction of the polls became approximately 16 percentage points more likely to correctly identify the lead party between the pre- and post-experiment surveys, and those who saw a textual description of the race became about 33 points more likely to do so. There was essentially no change for those in the control groups. Thus, there is evidence that respondents' factual information pertaining to the poll standings was shaped by treatment.[41] This suggests that the generally small effects of polls we estimated are not due to an outright absence of treatment uptake.

Second, are our estimated effects artificially weak because our platform fails to adequately mimic real elections, meaning it does not accurately capture the ways in which people might respond to opinion polls with regard to their information searches and vote choices? We cannot exclude this possibility with certainty. However, in previous applications of this platform, we have uncovered theoretically reasonable relationships between political sophistication and the information search (Roy et al. 2015), the information search and vote choice (Roy and Alcantara 2015; 2020; Roy et al. 2015; Singh and Roy 2014), reluctant voting under compulsory voting rules and the information search (Singh and Roy 2018), the number of competing parties and the information search (Roy and Singh 2012), and campaign negativity and the information search (Roy and Alcantara 2016; 2020). While it is true that our study takes place in an artificial setting, given the breadth of results that have conformed to expectations and theoretical grounding, we are confident in our platform's ability to capture how poll exposure affects real-world political behaviour.

Lastly, one might argue that our capacity to identify the true effects of polls could be dampened by motivated reasoning. Perhaps citizens who are already prone to vote for the party portrayed as leading the race are most likely to consider the polls to be credible, while those who prefer trailing parties dismiss them as false (Kuru, Pasek, and Traugott 2017). If this were the case, treatment uptake would be relatively strong among those who would select the frontrunner absent polls and relatively weak among those who are predisposed to vote against the party that is ahead. This would make it harder to detect evidence of a bandwagon effect and would bias toward an underdog effect. However, such a phenomenon should also apply to real-world polls, suggesting the effects we reveal are not particularly susceptible to motivated

---

[41] It is noteworthy that, while participants exposed to the stimulus updated their knowledge of poll standings, their perceptions of competitiveness were not affected by treatment. There was almost no difference across the control and treatment groups in their responses to the following question: "How competitive do you think the next Canadian federal election will be?" And, this is the case regardless of the mode of presentation: 80% of respondents in both the graphical control and treatment groups, 80% of those in the textual control group, and 78% of those in the textual treatment group felt the next election would be somewhat or very competitive. Thus, while our treatments changed people's factual information about the landscape, they apparently did not affect their perceptions of the competing parties' chances of success.

reasoning. Moreover, our investigations find that poll effects without actual party labels are no different from those with actual party labels, further evidencing against the influence of motivated reasoning. Finally, our results show that trust in polls does not moderate their influence on the information search and vote choice: the impact of polls is the same whether people deem them trustworthy or not.

5.3. Implications for Electoral Policy and Academic Research

As polls are often believed to be influential within and outside academia, our anaemic findings across ten studies in six countries are both sobering and consequential. Our analyses indicate polls have less of an influence on voter behaviour than many people think. They should alleviate the concerns of those who worry about how polls might sway the electorate. They also call into question the necessity of policies that prohibit the publication of pre-election polls. As we discuss in the first section, about two-fifths of countries impose a blackout on polls for some period during electoral campaigns. If polls have minimal effects on voters, as our results attest, then there is less justification for this type of media suppression, which has already faced and lost legal challenges in Bulgaria, Hungary, and Slovenia.

Still, we do marshal evidence that exposure to polls could alter election results in some instances. For example, parties trailing in the polls may lose additional support when the electorate is made aware of this. While the effect is small, slight shifts in support can translate into a nontrivial loss of seats in countries with proportional electoral systems. And, for small parties, such a decline could mean the difference between entering or being excluded from parliament. Even outside of proportional systems, small shifts in support could potentially make a big difference. For instance, a one-point shift in vote share toward the Liberal Party in the 2019 Canadian federal election could have produced a majority instead of a minority Liberal government. We also find a larger bandwagon effect of about four percentage points among voters who do not have a psychological attachment to a political party. This suggests that polls could more easily swing election results in competitions in which the voting public consists mostly of non-partisans.

What do our findings mean for academic research on poll effects? First, ours is one of very few studies to assess the impact of polls on voters' engagement with campaign information. Our discovery that exposure to polls decreases the information search (albeit slightly) may inform future work. Scholars who are interested in other ways polls may affect citizens, including outcomes like vote choice and political attitudes, should be aware that these links could be mediated by voters' divestment from political information gathering.

We also believe that future research should more rigorously study the impact of polls on the campaign strategies of political parties and candidates. Polls provide valuable information to parties and candidates by signalling their standing vis-à-vis their competitors. Indeed, it is well known that politicians pay attention to the polls, and they often conduct their own internal polling. However, with some notable exceptions (e.g., Geer 1996; Genovese and Streb 2005; Canes-Wrone 2006; Eisinger 2008), academic work on the relevance of polls for elites is comparatively underdeveloped. And, studies that do assess the relationship often rely on description and observation. A clever design that manages to randomize elites' exposure to polling information, perhaps with emails (see, for example, Butler and Broockman 2011), and subsequently measure changes in their behaviour would be extremely valuable.

We also believe our study is relevant for future observational research on individual-level poll effects. As we suggest in Section 1, relationships between poll exposure and political behaviours and attitudes based on observational data are likely biased upward by reverse causality (people who are more prone to a particular behaviour or attitude may, as a result, be more likely to view polls). Drawing exclusively from such data, with the additional challenges of unmeasured or omitted variables (certain types of people being more predisposed to particular behaviours or attitudes and also being more likely to view polls), may lead to overestimates of poll effects. It is our hope that the methodological approach and corresponding findings offered here help highlight these concerns.

Of course, most observational studies have one strong advantage over the web-based experimental design we employ: it is easier to generalize their results to the broader population. Future research might amalgamate the two approaches, randomizing individuals' exposure to polls in the "real world." This could be done at the macro-level by, for instance, randomly renting billboards in, or sending mailers to, different election wards or precincts. At the micro-level, it would be possible to randomly expose individuals to polls with targeted online ads or, again, mailers. It would then be possible to identify the real-world impacts of polls, in the macro case, by comparing ward- or precinct-level election returns, and, in the micro case, by analyzing validated voting data (the secret ballot in most places would mean only turnout could be analysed). The end result of these efforts would be credible estimates of the effects of poll exposure with a high degree of external validity. Our expectation is that such field experiments would identify only small effects of polls, as we did using an online experimental platform. Gerber and colleagues (2020) offer the first study along these lines, and they observe little evidence of an influence of polls on turnout.

Whether our results are confirmed or refuted, we hope that the findings we have presented here encourage future research to assess the impacts of public opinion polls on citizens. The importance of understanding the *power of polls* continues to grow in step with their increasingly dominant presence in election races around the globe.

References

Aalberg, T., Strömbäck, J., and de Vreese, C.H. (2012). "The framing of politics as strategy and game: A review of concepts, operationalizations and key findings." *Journalism*, 13(2), 162–178.

Abrams, M. (1970). "The opinion polls and the 1970 British general election." *Public Opinion Quarterly*, 34(3), 317–324.

Achen, C.H. and Bartels, L.M. (2017). *Democracy for realists: Why elections do not produce responsive government*. Princeton: Princeton University Press.

Agranov, M., Goeree, J., Romero, J., and Yariv, L. (2018). "What makes voters turn out: The effects of polls and beliefs." *Journal of the European Economic Association*, 16(3), 825–856.

Aldrich, J.H., Schober, G.S., Ley, S., and Fernandez, M. (2018). "Incognizance and perceptual deviation: Individual and institutional sources of variation in citizens' perceptions of party placements on the left-right scale." *Political Behavior*, 40(2), 415–433.

Alt, J.E., Marshall, J., and Lassen, D.D. (2016). "Credible sources and sophisticated voters: When does new information induce economic voting?" *Journal of Politics*, 78(2), 327–342.

Ansolabehere, S., and Iyengar, S. (1994). "Of horseshoes and horse races: Experimental studies of the impact of poll results on electoral behavior." *Political Communication*, 11(4), 413–430.

Apter, A.J., Wang, X., Bogen, D., Bennett, I.M., Jennings, R.M., Garcia, L., Sharpe, T., Frazier, C., and Have, T.T. (2009). "Linking numeracy and asthma-related quality of life." *Patient Education and Counseling*, 75(3), 386–391.

Arceneaux, K. and Kolodny, R. (2009). "Educating the least informed: Group endorsements in a grassroots campaign." *American Journal of Political Science*, 53(4), 55–77.

Arnold, J.R. (2012). "The electoral consequences of voter ignorance." *Electoral Studies*, 31(4): 796–815.

Baker, R., Blumberg, S.J., Brick, J.M., Couper, M.P., Courtright, M., Dennis, J. M., Dillman, D., Frankel, M.R., Garland, P., Groves, R.M., Kennedy, C., Krosnick, J., Lavrakas, P.J., Lee, S., Link, M., Piekarski, L., Rao, K., Thomas, R.K., and Zahs, D. (2010). "Research synthesis: AAPOR report on online panels", *Public Opinion Quarterly*, 74(4), 711–781.

Bakker, B.N., Lelkes, Y., and Malka, A. (2020). "Understanding partisan cue receptivity: Tests of predictions from the bounded rationality and expressive utility perspectives." *Journal of Politics*, 82(3),1061–1077.

Barabas, J., Jerit, J., Pollock, W., and Rainey, C. (2014). "The question(s) of political knowledge." *American Political Science Review*, 108(4), 840–855.

Bartels, L.M. (1985). "Expectations and preferences in presidential nominating campaigns." *American Political Science Review*, 79(3), 804–815.

Bartels, L.M. (1987). "Candidate choice and the dynamics of the presidential nominating process." *American Journal of Political Science*, 31(1), 1–30.

Bartels, L.M. (1988). *Presidential primaries and the dynamics of public choice.* Princeton: Princeton University Press.

Bartels, L.M. (1996). "Uninformed votes: Information effects in presidential elections." *American Journal of Political Science*, 40(1), 194–230.

Bartels, L.M. (2000). "Partisanship and voting behavior, 1952–1996." *American Journal of Political Science*, 44(1), 35–50.

Bartels, L.M. (2002). "Beyond the running tally: Partisan bias in political perceptions." *Political Behavior*, 24(2), 117–150.

Beniger, J.R. (1976). "Winning the presidential nomination: National polls and state primary elections, 1936–1972." *Public Opinion Quarterly*, 40(1), 22–38.

Bennion, E.A. (2005). "Caught in the ground wars: Mobilizing voters during a competitive congressional campaign." *The Annals of the American Academy of Political and Social Science*, 601(1), 123–141.

Berelson, B.R., Lazarsfeld, P.F., and McPhee, W.N. (1954). *Voting: A study of opinion formation in a presidential campaign.* Chicago: University of Chicago Press.

Bhatti, Y. (2010). "What would happen if we were better informed? Simulating increased knowledge in European Parliament (EP) elections." *Representation*, 46(4), 391–410.

Biggers, D.R., Hendry, D.J., Gerber, A.A., and Huber, G.A. (2017). "Experimental evidence about whether (and why) electoral closeness affects turnout." Unpublished manuscript.

Binning, K.R., Brick, C., Cohen, G.L., and Sherman, D.K. (2015). "Going along versus getting it right: The role of self-integrity in political conformity." *Journal of Experimental Social Psychology*, 56(1), 73–88.

Bischoff, I. and Egbert, H. (2013). "Social information and bandwagon behavior in voting: An economic experiment." *Journal of Economic Psychology*, 34(1), 270–284.

Bisgaard, M. and Slothuus, R. (2018). "Partisan elites as culprits? How party cues shape partisan perceptual gaps." *American Journal of Political Science*, 62(2), 456–469.

Blais, A. (2000). *To vote or not to vote?: The merits and limits of rational choice theory.* Pittsburgh: University of Pittsburgh Press.

Blais, A. (2006). "What affects voter turnout?" *Annual Review of Political Science*, 9, 111–125.

Blais, A. and Bodet, M.A. (2006). "How do voters form expectations about the parties' chances of winning the election?" *Social Science Quarterly*, 87(3), 477–493.

Blais, A., Gidengil, E., and Nevitte, N. (2006). "Do polls influence the vote?" in Brady H. & Johnston R. (eds.), *Capturing campaign effects*. Ann Arbor: University of Michigan Press, 263–279.

Blais, A., Gidengil, E., Fournier, P., and Nevitte, N. (2009). "Information, visibility and elections: Why electoral outcomes differ when voters are better informed." *European Journal of Political Research*, 48(2), 256–280.

Blais, A., Gidengil, E., Nadeau, R., and Nevitte, N. (2001). "Measuring party identification: Britain, Canada, and the United States." *Political Behavior*, 23 (1), 5–22.

Blais, A., Gidengil, E., Nadeau, R., and Nevitte, N. (2002). *Anatomy of a Liberal victory.* Peterborough: Broadview Press.

Blais, A., Loewen, P.J., Rubenson, D., Stephenson, L.B., and Gidengil, E. (2018). "Information on party strength and strategic voting." in L. B. Stephenson, J.H. Aldrich & A. Blais (eds.), *The many faces of strategic voting*, Ann Arbor: University of Michigan Press, 89–103.

Blais, A., Vowles, J., and Aarts, K. (2002). "Does the impact of polls vary across electoral systems?" Presented at the Annual Meeting of the American Political Science Association, Boston.

Bosch, A. and Orriols, L. (2014). "Ballot structure and satisfaction with democracy." *Journal of Elections, Public Opinion & Parties*, 24(4), 493–511.

Boudreau, C. and McCubbins, M.D. (2010). "The blind leading the blind: Who gets polling information and does it improve decisions?" *Journal of Politics*, 72(2), 513–527.

Brady, H.E. and Johnston, R. (1987). "What's the primary message: Horse race or issue journalism?" In G. Orren and N. Polsby (eds.), *Media and Momentum*. Chatham, NJ: Chatham House, 127–86.

Brettschneider, F. (1997). "The press and the polls in Germany, 1980–1994 poll coverage as an essential part of election campaign reporting." *International Journal of Public Opinion Research*, 9(3), 248–265.

Broh, C.A. (1980). "Horse-race journalism: Reporting the polls in the 1976 presidential election." *Public Opinion Quarterly*, 44(4), 514–529.

Buchanan, W. (1986). "Election predictions: An empirical assessment." *Public Opinion Quarterly*, 50(2), 222–227.

Burden, B.C. (2005). "Minor parties and strategic voting in recent US presidential elections." *Electoral Studies*, 24(4), 603–618.

Butler, D.M. and Broockman, D.E. (2011). "Do politicians racially discriminate against constituents? A field experiment on state legislators." *American Journal of Political Science*, 55(3), 463–77.

Bursztyn, L., Cantoni, D., Funk, P., and Yuchtman, N. (2017). "Polls, the press, and political participation: The effects of anticipated election closeness on voter turnout." Working Paper No. 23490. National Bureau of Economic Research.

Callegaro, M., Baker, R.P., Bethlehem, J., Göritz, A.S., Krosnick, J.A., and Lavrakas, P.J. (2014). *Online panel research: A data quality perspective.* Chichester: John Wiley & Sons.

Campbell, A., Converse, P.E., Miller, W.E., and Stokes, D.E. (1960). *The American voter.* Chicago: University of Chicago Press.

Cancela, J., and Geys, B. (2016). "Explaining voter turnout: A meta-analysis of national and subnational elections." *Electoral Studies*, 42(1), 264–275.

Canes-Wrone, B. (2006). *Who leads whom? Presidents, policy, and the public.* Chicago: University of Chicago Press.

Carroll, R. and Kubo, H. (2018). "Explaining citizen perceptions of party ideological positions: The mediating role of political contexts." *Electoral Studies*, 5(1), 14–23.

Cavanaugh, K., Huizinga, M.M., Wallston, K.A., Gebretsadik, T., Shintani, A., Davis, D., Gregory, R.P., et al. (2008). "Association of numeracy and diabetes control." *Annals of Internal Medicine*, 148(10), 737–746.

Ceci, S.J. and Kain, E.L. (1982). "Jumping on the bandwagon with the underdog: The impact of attitude polls on polling behavior." *Public Opinion Quarterly*, 46(2), 228–242.

Choma, B.L., Sumantry, D., and Hanoch, Y. (2019). "Right-wing ideology and numeracy: A perception of greater ability, but poorer performance." *Judgment & Decision Making*, 14(4), 412–422.

Chung, S., Heo, Y., and Moon, J. (2018). "Perceived versus actual polling effects: Biases in perceptions of election poll effects on candidate evaluations." *International Journal of Public Opinion Research*, 30(3), 420–442.

Cloutier, E., Nadeau, R., and Guay, J.H. (1989). "Bandwagoning and underdoging on North- American free trade: A quasi-experimental panel study of opinion movement." *International Journal of Public Opinion Research*, 1(3), 206–220.

Coddington, M. (2015). "Clarifying journalism's quantitative turn: A typology for evaluating data journalism, computational journalism, and computer-assisted reporting." *Digital Journalism*, 3(3), 331–348.

Converse , P. E . (1964). "The nature and belief systems in mass publics." In D. Apter (ed.), *Ideology and Discontent*. New York: Free Press, 206–261.

Cook, S.A. and Welch, A.C. (1940). "Methods of measuring the practical effects of polls of public opinion." *Journal of Applied Psychology*, 24(4), 441–454.

Craig, J. (2018). "The promises of numeracy." *Educational Studies in Mathematics*, 99(1), 57–71.

Craig, R. (2000). "Expectations and elections: How television defines campaign news." *Critical Studies in Media Communication*, 17(1), 28–44.

Crewe, I. (2005). "The opinion polls: The election they got (almost) right." *Parliamentary Affairs*, 58(4), 684–698.

Curtice, J. (1997). "So how well did they do? The polls in the 1997 election." *International Journal of Market Research*, 39(3), 449–461.

Cox, G.W. and Munger, M.C. (1989). "Closeness, expenditures, and turnout in the 1982 US House elections." *American Political Science Review*, 83(1), 217–231.

Dahlgaard, J.O., Hansen, J.H., Hansen, K.M., and Larsen, M.V. (2017). "How election polls shape voting behaviour." *Scandinavian Political Studies*, 40 (3), 330–343.

Dale, A. and Strauss, A. (2009). "Don't forget to vote: Text message reminders as a mobilization tool." *American Journal of Political Science*, 53(4), 787–804.

Daschmann, G. (2000). "Vox pop & polls: The impact of poll results and voter statements in the media on the perception of a climate of opinion." *International Journal of Public Opinion Research*, 12(2), 160–181.

Dassonneville, R. (Forthcoming). *Under Pressure: Group-Based Cross-Pressure and Voter Volatility*. Oxford: Oxford University Press.

Dassonneville, R. and McAllister, I. (2018). "Gender, political knowledge, and descriptive representation: The impact of long-term socialization." *American Journal of Political Science*, 62(2), 249–265.

de Bock, H. (1976). "Influence of in-state election poll reports on candidate preference in 1972." *Journalism Quarterly*, 53(3), 457–462.

Delli Carpini, M.X. (1984). "Scooping the voters? The consequences of the networks' early call of the 1980 presidential race." *Journal of Politics*, 46(3), 866–885.

Delli Carpini, M.X., and Keeter, S. (1993). "Measuring political knowledge: Putting first things first." *American Journal of Political Science*, 37(4), 1179–1206.

Delli Carpini, M.X., and Keeter, S. (1996). *What Americans know about politics and why it matters*. New Haven: Yale University Press.

Dieckmann, N.F., Slovic, P., and Peters, M.E. (2009). "The use of narrative evidence and explicit likelihood by decisionmakers varying in numeracy." *Risk Analysis: An International Journal*, 29(10), 1473–1488.

Dimitrova, D.V. and Kostadinova, P. (2013). "Identifying antecedents of the strategic game frame: A longitudinal analysis." *Journalism & Mass Communication Quarterly*, 90(1), 75–88.

Downs, A. (1957). *An economic theory of democracy*. New York: Harper.

Druckman, J.N. (2001). "On the limits of framing effects: Who can frame?" *Journal of Politics*, 63(4), 1041–1066.

Druckman, J.N. and Nelson, K.R. (2003). "Framing and deliberation: How citizens' conversations limit elite influence." *American Journal of Political Science*, 47(4), 729–745.

DuBois, P.L. (1983). "Election night projections and voter turnout in the west: A note on the hazards of aggregate data analysis." *American Politics Research*, 11(3), 349–64.

Dunaway, J. and Lawrence, R.G. (2015). "What predicts the game frame? Media ownership, electoral context, and campaign news." *Political Communication*, 32(1), 43–60.

Durand, C., Blais, A., and Larochelle, M. (2004). "The polls in the 2002 French presidential election: An autopsy." *Public Opinion Quarterly*, 68(4), 602–622.

Eisinger, R.M. (2008). "The use of surveys by governments and politicians." in Wolfgang D. and Traugott, M.W. (eds.), *The SAGE handbook of public opinion research*. London: SAGE Publications, 487–95.

Enos, R.D. and Fowler, A. (2014). "Pivotality and turnout: Evidence from a field experiment in the aftermath of a tied election." *Political Science Research and Methods*, 2(2), 309–319.

Epstein, L.K. and Strom, G. (1981). "Election night projections and west coast turnout." *American Politics Quarterly*, 9(4), 479–491.

Erikson, R.S. and Sigelman, L. (1995). "Poll-based forecasts of midterm congressional election outcomes: Do the pollsters get it right?" *Public Opinion Quarterly*, 59(4), 589–605.

Erikson, R.S. and Wlezien, C. (2012). *The timeline of presidential elections: How campaigns do (and do not) matter*. Chicago: University of Chicago Press.

Estrada-Mejia, C., De Vries, M., and Zeelenberg, M. (2016). "Numeracy and wealth." *Journal of Economic Psychology*, 54(1), 53–63.

Farjam, M. (Forthcoming). "The bandwagon effect in an online voting experiment with real political organizations." *International Journal of Public Opinion Research*.

Federico, C.M. and Hunt, C.V. (2013). "Political information, political involvement, and reliance on ideology in political evaluation." *Political Behavior*, 35(1), 89–112.

Felson, M. and Sudman, S. (1975). "The accuracy of presidential preference primary polls." *Public Opinion Quarterly*, 39(2), 232–236.

Fisher, S.D., Lessard-Phillips, L., Hobolt, S.B., and Curtice, J. (2008). "Disengaging voters: Do plurality systems discourage the less knowledgeable from voting?" *Electoral Studies*, 27(1), 89–104.

Fiske, S.T., Kinder, D.R., and Larter, W.M. (1983). "The novice and the expert: Knowledge-based strategies in political cognition." *Journal of Experimental Social Psychology*, 19(4), 381–400.

Fiske, S.T and Taylor, S.E. (1991). *Social cognition*. New York: Mcgraw-Hill Book Company.

Fleitas, D.W. (1971). "Bandwagon and underdog effects in minimal-information elections." *American Political Science Review*, 65(2), 434–438.

Forsythe, R., Myerson, R.B., Rietz, T.A., and Weber, R.J. (1993). "An experiment on coordination in multi-candidate elections: The importance of polls and election histories." *Social Choice and Welfare*, 10(3), 223–247.

Fortunato, D. and Stevenson, R.T. (2013). "Perceptions of partisan ideologies: The effect of coalition participation." *American Journal of Political Science*, 57(2), 459–477.

Fournier, P. (2006). "The impact of campaigns on discrepancies, errors, and biases in voting behavior." in Brady H. & Johnston R. (eds.), *Capturing campaign effects*. Ann Arbor: University of Michigan Press, 45–77.

Fournier, P., Cutler, F., and Soroka, S. (2019). "Who responds to election campaigns? The two-moderator model revisited." in P. Loewen and D. Rubenson (eds.), *Duty and choice: The evolution of the study of voting and voters*. Toronto: University of Toronto Press, 129–168.

Fowler, A. and Margolis, M. (2014). "The political consequences of uninformed voters." *Electoral Studies*, 34(1), 100–110.

Fraile, M. and Gomez, R. (2017). "Bridging the enduring gender gap in political interest in Europe: The relevance of promoting gender equality." *European Journal of Political Research*, 56(3), 601–618.

Fredén, A. (2017). "Opinion polls, coalition signals and strategic voting: Evidence from a survey experiment." *Scandinavian Political Studies*, 40(3), 247–264.

Fuchs, D.A. (1966). "Election-day radio-television and western voting." *Public Opinion Quarterly*, 30(2), 226–236.

Gaines, B.J., Kuklinski, J.H., Quirk, P.J., Peyton, B., and Verkuilen, J. (2007). "Same facts, different interpretations: Partisan motivation and opinion on Iraq." *Journal of Politics*, 69(4), 957–974.

Geer, J.G. (1996). *From tea leaves to opinion polls: A theory of democratic leadership*. New York: Columbia University Press.

Genovese, M.A. and Streb, M.J. (2005). *Polls and politics: The dilemmas of democracy*. Albany: State University of New York Press.

Gerber, A.S., Huber, G.A., and Washington, E. (2010). "Party affiliation, partisanship, and political beliefs: A field experiment." *American Political Science Review*, 104(4), 720–744.

Gerber, A.S. and Green, D.P. (2000). "The effects of canvassing, telephone calls, and direct mail on voter turnout: A field experiment." *American Political Science Review*, 94(3), 653–663.

Gerber, A., Hoffman, M., Morgan, J., and Raymond, C. (2020). "One in a million: Field experiments on perceived closeness of the election and voter turnout." *American Economic Journal: Applied Economics*, 12(3), 287–325.

Geys, B. (2006). "Explaining voter turnout: A review of aggregate-level research." *Electoral Studies*, 25(4), 637–663.

Giammo, J.D. (2004). "Polls and voting behavior: The impact of polling information on candidate preference, turnout, and strategic voting." Doctoral Dissertation. University of Texas, Austin.

Gidengil, E., Blais, A., Nevitte, N., and Nadeau, R. (2004). *Citizens*. Vancouver: UBC Press.

Gidengil, E., Blais, A., Everitt, J., Fournier, P., and Nevitte, N. (2012). *Dominance and decline: Making sense of recent Canadian elections*. Toronto: University of Toronto Press.

Gimpel, J.G. and Harvey, D.H. (1997). "Forecasts and preferences in the 1992 general election." *Political Behavior*, 19(2), 157–175.

Glynn, C.J., Hayes, A.F., and Shanahan, J. (1997). "Perceived support for one's opinions and willingness to speak out: A meta-analysis of survey studies on the 'Spiral of Silence'." *Public Opinion Quarterly*, 61(3), 452–463.

Glynn, C.J. and Huge, M.E. (2014). "Speaking in spirals: An updated meta-analysis of the spiral of silence." in W. Donsbach, C.T. Salmon & Y. Tsfati (eds.), *The spiral of silence*. New York: Routledge, 81–88.

Goot, M. (2010). "Underdogs, bandwagons or incumbency? Party support at the beginning and the end of Australian election campaigns, 1983–2007." *Australian Cultural History*, 28(1), 69–80.

Gordon, S.B. and Segura, G.M. (1997). "Cross-national variation in the political sophistication of individuals: Capability or choice?" *Journal of Politics*, 59(1), 126–147.

Gosnell, H.F. (1937). "Technical research: How accurate were the polls?" *Public Opinion Quarterly*, 1(1), 97–105.

Green, D.P., Palmquist, B., and Schickler, E. (2004). *Partisan hearts and minds: Political parties and the social identities of voters*. New Haven: Yale University Press.

Großer, J. and Schram, A. (2010). "Public opinion polls, voter turnout, and welfare: An experimental study." *American Journal of Political Science*, 54(3), 700–17.

Hansen, K.M. (2009). "Changing patterns in the impact of information on party choice in a multiparty system." *International Journal of Public Opinion Research*, 21(4), 525–546.

Hart, P.S. (2013). "The role of numeracy in moderating the influence of statistics in climate change messages." *Public Understanding of Science*, 22(7), 785–798.

Hayes, A.F. (2007). "Exploring the forms of self-censorship: On the spiral of silence and the use of opinion expression avoidance strategies." *Journal of Communication*, 57(4), 785–802.

Hovland, C.I. and Weiss, W. (1951). "The influence of source credibility on communication effectiveness." *Public Opinion Quarterly*, 15(4), 635–650.

Huang, H. (2005). "A cross-cultural test of the spiral of silence." *International Journal of Public Opinion Research*, 17(3), 324–345.

Irwin, G.A. and Van Holsteyn, J.J.M. (2002). "According to the polls: The influence of opinion polls on expectations." *Public Opinion Quarterly*, 66(1), 92–104.

Ismagilova, E., Slade, E., Rana, N.P., and Dwivedi, Y.K. (2020). "The effect of characteristics of source credibility on consumer behaviour: A meta-analysis." *Journal of Retailing and Consumer Services*, 53, 101736.

Iyengar, S., Norpoth, H., and Hahn, K.S. (2004). "Consumer demand for election news: The horserace sells." *Journal of Politics*, 66(1), 157–175.

Jackson, J.E. (1983). "Election night reporting and voter turnout." *American Journal of Political Science*, 27(4), 615–35.

Jacoby, W.G. (2009). "Ideology and vote choice in the 2004 election." *Electoral Studies*, 28(4), 584–594.

Jennings, W. (2019). "The polls in 2017." in D. Wring, R. Mortimore, & S. Atkinson (eds.), *Political communication in Britain: Campaigning, media and polling in the 2017 general election*. Basingstoke, UK: Palgrave Macmillan, 209–220.

Jennings, W. and Wlezien, C. (2018). "Election polling errors across time and space." *Nature Human Behaviour* 2(4), 276–283.

Jerit, J. and Barabas, J. (2012). "Partisan perceptual bias and the information environment." *Journal of Politics*, 74(3), 672–684.

Jessee, S.A. (2009). "Spatial voting in the 2004 presidential election." *American Political Science Review*, 103(1), 59–81.

Jessee, S.A. (2010). "Partisan bias, political information and spatial voting in the 2008 presidential election." *Journal of Politics*, 72(2), 327–340.

Johnston, R., Blais, A., Brady, H., and Crête, J. (1992). *Letting the people decide: Dynamics of a Canadian election*, Montreal: McGill-Queen's Press.

Johnston, R., Blais, A., Gidengil, E., and Nevitte, N. (1996). *Challenge of direct democracy: The 1992 Canadian referendum*. Montreal: McGill-Queen's Press.

Jowell, R., Hedges, B., Lynn, P., Farrant, G., and Heath, A. (1993). "The 1992 British election: the failure of the polls." *Public Opinion Quarterly*, 57(2), 238–263.

Julious, S. A. (2004). "Using confidence intervals around individual means to assess statistical significance between two means." *Pharmaceutical Statistics*, 3(3), 217–22.

Kahan, D.M. (2012). "Ideology, motivated reasoning, and cognitive reflection: An experimental study." *Judgment and Decision Making*, 8(4), 407–24.

Kahneman, D. (2011). *Thinking, fast and slow*. New York: Macmillan.

Kam, C.D. (2005). "Who toes the party line? Cues, values, and individual differences." *Political Behavior*, 27(2), 163–182.

Kam, C.D. and Utych, S.M. (2011). "Close elections and cognitive engagement." *Journal of Politics*, 73(4), 1251–1266.

Kam, C.D. and Trussler, M.J. (2017). "At the nexus of observational and experimental research: Theory, specification, and analysis of experiments with heterogeneous treatment effects." *Political Behavior*, 39(4), 789–815.

Katz, C. and Baldassare, M. (1992). "Using the 'L-word' in public: A test of the spiral of silence in conservative Orange County, California." *Public Opinion Quarterly*, 56(2), 232–235.

Katz, C. and Baldassare, M. (1994). "Popularity in a freefall: Measuring a spiral of silence at the end of the Bush presidency." *International Journal of Public Opinion Research*, 6(1), 1–12.

Kennedy, C., Blumenthal, M., Clement, S., Clinton, J.D., Durand, C., Franklin, C., McGeeney, K., et al. (2018). "An evaluation of the 2016 election polls in the United States." *Public Opinion Quarterly*, 82(1), 1–33.

Kenney, P.J., and Rice, T.W. (1994). "The psychology of political momentum." *Political Research Quarterly*, 47(4), 923–938.

Kittilson, M.C. and Schwindt-Bayer, L. (2010). "Engaging citizens: The role of power-sharing institutions." *Journal of Politics*, 72(4), 990–1002.

Klor, E.F. and Winter, E. (2018). "On public opinion polls and voters' turnout." *Journal of Public Economic Theory*, 20(2), 239–256.

Krosnick, J.A. and Brannon, L.A. (1993). "The impact of the Gulf War on the ingredients of presidential evaluations: Multidimensional effects of political involvement." *American Political Science Review*, 87(4), 963–975.

Kuru, O., Pasek, J., and Traugott, M.W. (2017). "Motivated reasoning in the perceived credibility of public opinion polls." *Public Opinion Quarterly*, 81(2), 422–46.

Kutner, M., Greenburg, E., Jin, Y., and Paulsen, C. (2006). "The health literacy of America's adults: Results from the 2003 national assessment of adult literacy. NCES 2006–483." *National Center for Education Statistics*.

Lang, K. and Lang, G.E. (1968). *Voting and nonvoting: Implications of broadcasting returns before polls are closed.* Waltham: Blaisdell Publishing Company.

Larcinese, V. (2007). "Does political knowledge increase turnout? Evidence from the 1997 British general election." *Public Choice*, 131(3–4), 387–411.

Lasorsa, D.L. (1991). "Political outspokenness: Factors working against the spiral of silence." *Journalism Quarterly*, 68(1–2), 131–140.

Lassen, D.D. (2005). "The effect of information on voter turnout: Evidence from a natural experiment." *American Journal of Political Science*, 49(1), 103–118.

Lau, R.R., Andersen, D.J., and Redlawsk, D.P. (2008). "An exploration of correct voting in recent US presidential elections." *American Journal of Political Science*, 52(2), 395–411.

Lau, R.R. and Redlawsk, D.P. (2001). "Advantages and disadvantages of cognitive heuristics in political decision making." *American Journal of Political Science*, 45(4), 951–971.

Lau, R.R., Patel, P., Fahmy, D.F., and Kaufman, R.R. (2014). "Correct voting across thirty-three democracies: A preliminary analysis." *British Journal of Political Science*, 44(2), 239–259.

Laustsen, L. and Petersen, M.B. (2016). "Winning faces vary by ideology: How nonverbal source cues influence election and communication success in politics." *Political Communication*, 33(2), 188–211.

Lengauer, G., and Höller, I. (2012). "Contest framing and its effects on voter (de) mobilisation: News exposure and its impact on voting turnout in the 2008 Austrian elections." *Javnost-The Public*, 19(4), 73–91.

Lipkus, I.M., Samsa, G., and Rimer, B.K. (2001). "General performance on a numeracy scale among highly educated samples." *Medical Decision Making*, 21(1), 37–44.

Lodge, M. and Taber, C.S. (2013). *The rationalizing voter.* Cambridge: Cambridge University Press.

Lupia, A. (1994). "Shortcuts versus encyclopedias: Information and voting behavior in California insurance reform elections." *American Political Science Review*, 88(1), 63–76.

Lusardi, A. and Mitchell, O.S. (2007). "Baby boomer retirement security: The roles of planning, financial literacy, and housing wealth." *Journal of Monetary Economics*, 54(1), 205–224.

Luskin, R.C. (1987). "Measuring political sophistication." *American Journal of Political Science*, 31(4), 856–899.

Luskin, R.C. (1990). "Explaining political sophistication." *Political Behavior*, 12(4), 331–361.

Magalhães, P.C. (2005). "Pre-election polls in Portugal: Accuracy, bias, and sources of error, 1991–2004." *International Journal of Public Opinion Research*, 17(4), 399–421.

Malka, A. and Lelkes, Y. (2010). "More than ideology: Conservative–liberal identity and receptivity to political cues." *Social Justice Research*, 23(2–3), 156–188.

Marsh, C. (1985). "Back on the bandwagon: The effect of opinion polls on public opinion." *British Journal of Political Science*, 15(1), 51–74.

Matthes, J. (2015). "Observing the 'spiral' in the spiral of silence." *International Journal of Public Opinion Research*, 27(2), 155–176.

Matthes, J., Morrison, K.R., and Schemer, C. (2010). "A spiral of silence for some: Attitude certainty and the expression of political minority opinions." *Communication Research*, 37(6), 774–800.

Matthes, J., Knoll, J., and von Sikorski, C. (2018). "The 'spiral of silence' revisited: A meta-analysis on the relationship between perceptions of opinion support and political opinion expression." *Communication Research*, 45(1), 3–33.

Mayne, Q. and Hakhverdian, A. (2017). "Ideological congruence and citizen satisfaction: Evidence from 25 advanced democracies." *Comparative Political Studies*, 50(6), 822–849.

McAllister, I. and Studlar, D.T. (1991). "Bandwagon, underdog, or projection? Opinion polls and electoral choice in Britain, 1979–1987." *Journal of Politics*, 53(3), 720–741.

McDermott, R. (2011). "Internal and external validity." in J.N. Druckman, D. P. Green, J.H. Kuklinski & A. Lupia (eds.), *Cambridge handbook of experimental political science*, Cambridge: Cambridge University Press, 27–40.

McDonald, D.G., Glynn, C.J., Kim, S., and Ostman, R.E. (2001). "The spiral of silence in the 1948 presidential election." *Communication Research*, 28(2), 139–155.

McKelvey, R.D. and Ordeshook, P.C. (1985). "Elections with limited information: A fulfilled expectations model using contemporaneous poll and endorsement data as information sources." *Journal of Economic Theory*, 36(1), 55–85.

Meffert, M.F. and Gschwend, T. (2011). "Polls, coalition signals and strategic voting: An experimental investigation of perceptions and effects." *European Journal of Political Research* 50(5), 636–667.

Mendelsohn, H. (1966). "Western voting and broadcasts of results on presidential election day." *Public Opinion Quarterly*, 30(2), 212–225.

Mendelsohn, H.A. and Crespi, I. (1970). *Polls, television, and the new politics*. Scranton: Chandler House Press.

Mendelsohn, M. (1993). "Television's frames in the 1988 Canadian election." *Canadian Journal of Communication*, 18(2), 149–171.

Mérola, V. and Hitt, M.P. (2016). "Numeracy and the persuasive effect of policy information and party cues." *Public Opinion Quarterly*, 80(2), 554–562.

Merolla, J.L. (2009). "The effect of information signals on strategic voting in mock mayoral elections." *Political Behavior*, 31(3), 379–399.

Miller, J.M. and Krosnick, J.A. (2000). "News media impact on the ingredients of presidential evaluations: Politically knowledgeable citizens are guided by a trusted source." *American Journal of Political Science*, 44(2), 301–315.

Miller, P.R. (2011). "The emotional citizen: emotion as a function of political sophistication." *Political Psychology*, 32(4), 575–600.

Mitchell, D. (2012). "It's about time: The lifespan of information effects in a multiweek campaign." *American Journal of Political Science*, 56(2), 298–311.

Mitofsky, W.J. (1998). "Was 1996 a worse year for polls than 1948?" *Public Opinion Quarterly*, 62(2), 230–249.

Mondak, J.J. (2001). "Developing valid knowledge scales." *American Journal of Political Science*, 45(1), 224–238.

Morton, R.B., Muller, D., Page, L., and Benno, T. (2015). "Exit polls, turnout, and bandwagon voting: Evidence from a natural experiment." *European Economic Review*, 77(1), 65–81.

Mosteller, F., Hyman, H., McCarthy, P.J., Marks, E.S., and Truman, D.B. (1949). *The pre-election polls of 1948: Report to the committee on analysis of pre-election polls and forecasts*. New York: Social Science Research Council.

Mutz, D.C. (1992). "Impersonal influence: Effects of representations of public opinion on political attitudes." *Political Behavior*, 14(2), 89–122.

Mutz, D.C. (1998). *Impersonal influence: How perceptions of mass collectives affect political attitudes*. Cambridge: Cambridge University Press.

Mutz, D.C. and Pemantle, R. (2015). "Standards for experimental research: Encouraging a better understanding of experimental methods." *Journal of Experimental Political Science*, 2(2), 192–215.

Nadeau, R., Cloutier, E., and Guay, J.H. (1993). "New evidence about the existence of a bandwagon effect in the opinion formation process." *International Political Science Review*, 14(2), 203–213.

Navazio, R. (1977). "An experimental approach to bandwagon research." *Public Opinion Quarterly*, 41(2), 217–225.

Nicholson, S.P. (2012). "Polarizing cues." *American Journal of Political Science*, 56(1), 52–66.

Niemi, R.G., Iusi, G. and Bianco, W. (1983). "Pre-election polls and turnout." *Journalism Quarterly*, 60(3), 530–533.

Noëlle-Neumann, E. (1974). "The spiral of silence a theory of public opinion." *Journal of Communication*, 24(2), 43–51.

Noëlle-Neumann, E. (1993). *The spiral of silence: Public opinion, our social skin*. Chicago: University of Chicago Press.

Oscarsson, H. (2007). "A matter of fact? Knowledge effects on the vote in Swedish general elections, 1985–2002." *Scandinavian Political Studies*, 30(3), 301–322.

Panagopoulos, C. (2009). "Polls and elections: Preelection poll accuracy in the 2008 general elections." *Presidential Studies Quarterly*, 39(4), 896–907.

Panagopoulos, C. and Farrer, B. (2014). "Polls and elections: Preelection poll accuracy and bias in the 2012 general elections." *Presidential Studies Quarterly*, 44(2), 352–363.

Patterson T.E. (1993). *Out of order*. New York: Random House.

Paulos, J.A. (1988). *Innumeracy: Mathematical illiteracy and its consequences*. New York: Hill and Wang.

Peters, E. and Levin, I.P. (2008). "Dissecting the risky-choice framing effect: Numeracy as an individual-difference factor in weighting risky and riskless options." *Judgment and Decision Making*, 3(6), 435–448.

Peters, E., Västfjäll, D., Slovic, P., Mertz, C.K., Mazzocco, K., and Dickert, S. (2006). "Numeracy and decision making." *Psychological Science*, 17(5), 407–413.

Petersen, M.B., Skov, M., Serritzlew, S., and Ramsøy, T. (2013). "Motivated reasoning and political parties: Evidence for increased processing in the face of party cues." *Political Behavior*, 35(4), 831–854.

Petty, R.E. and Wegener, D.T. (1998). "Attitude change: Multiple roles for persuasion variables." in D.T. Gilbert, S.T. Fiske, and G. Lindzey (eds.), *The handbook of social psychology*. Boston: McGraw-Hill, 323–90.

Pons, V. and Tricaud, C. (2019). "Coordination and bandwagon effects of candidate rankings: Evidence from runoff elections." Working Paper No. 26599. National Bureau of Economic Research.

Popkin, S.L. (1991). *The reasoning voter: Communication and persuasion in presidential campaigns*. Chicago: University of Chicago Press.

Pornpitakpan, C. (2004). "The persuasiveness of source credibility: A critical review of five decades' evidence." *Journal of Applied Social Psychology*, 34(2), 243–281.

Rapeli, L. (2018). "Does sophistication affect electoral outcomes?" *Government and Opposition*, 53(2), 181–204.

Reyna, V.F., Nelson, W.L., Han, P.K., and Dieckmann, N.F. (2009). "How numeracy influences risk comprehension and medical decision making." *Psychological Bulletin*, 135(6), 943–973.

Rich, T.S. (2015). "Strategic voting and the role of polls: Evidence from an embedded web survey." *PS: Political Science & Politics*, 48(2), 301–305.

Riker, W.H. and Ordeshook, P.C. (1968). "A theory of the calculus of voting." *American Political Science Review*, 62(1), 25–42.

Rios, K. and Chen, Z. (2014). "Experimental evidence for minorities' hesitancy in reporting their opinions: The roles of optimal distinctiveness needs and normative influence." *Personality and Social Psychology Bulletin*, 40(7), 872–883.

Rothschild, D. and Malhotra, N. (2014). "Are public opinion polls self-fulfilling prophecies?" *Research & Politics*, 1(2), 1–10.

Roy, J. (2011). "Information heterogeneity, complexity and the vote calculus." *Journal of Elections, Public Opinion and Parties*, 21(1), 29–56.

Roy, J. and Alcantara, C. (2020). *Winning and keeping power in Canadian politics*. Toronto: University of Toronto Press.

Roy, J. and Alcantara, C. (2016). "Fighting fire with fire: The implications of (not) going negative in a multiparty election campaign." *Canadian Journal of Political Science*, 49(3), 473–97.

Roy, J. and Alcantara, C. (2015). "The candidate effect: Does the local candidate matter?" *Journal of Elections, Public Opinion and Parties*, 25(2), 195–214.

Roy, J. and Singh, S.P. (2012). "Canadian and American voting strategies: Does institutional socialization matter?" *Canadian Journal of Political Science*, 45(2), 289–312.

Roy, J., Singh, S.P., Fournier, P., and Andrew, B. (2015). "An experimental analysis of the impact of campaign polls on electoral information seeking." *Electoral Studies*, 40(1), 146–57.

Sanders, D. (2003). "Pre-election polling in Britain, 1950–1997." *Electoral Studies*, 22(1), 1–20.

Schmitt-Beck, R. (1996). "Mass media, the electorate, and the bandwagon. A study of communication effects on vote choice in Germany." *International Journal of Public Opinion Research*, 8(3), 266–291.

Schmuck, D., Heiss, R., Matthes, J., Engesser, S. and Esser, F. (2017). "Antecedents of strategic game framing in political news coverage." *Journalism*, 18(8), 937–955.

Schuck, A., Vliegenthart, R., Hajo, G., Boomgaarden, M.E., Azrout, R., van Spanje, J., and de Vreese, C.H. (2013). "Explaining campaign news coverage: How medium, time, and context explain variation in the media framing of the 2009 European parliamentary elections." *Journal of Political Marketing*, 12(1), 8–28.

Schwartz, L.M., Woloshin, S., Black, W.C., and Welch, H.G. (1997). "The role of numeracy in understanding the benefit of screening mammography." *Annals of Internal Medicine*, 127(11), 966–972.

Shamir, J. (1997). "Speaking up and silencing out in face of a changing climate of opinion." *Journalism & Mass Communication Quarterly*, 74(3), 602–614.

Sigelman, L. and Bullock, D. (1991). "Candidates, issues, horse races, and hoopla: Presidential campaign coverage, 1888–1988." *American Politics Quarterly*, 19(1), 5–32.

Simon, H.A. (1954). "Bandwagon and underdog effects and the possibility of election predictions." *Public Opinion Quarterly*, 18(3), 245–253.

Sinclair, B. and Plott, C.R. (2012). "From uninformed to informed choices: Voters, pre-election polls and updating." *Electoral Studies*, 31(1), 83–95.

Singh, S.P. and Roy, J. (2014). "Political knowledge, the decision calculus, and proximity voting." *Electoral Studies*, 34(1), 89–99.

Singh, S.P. and Roy, J. (2018). "Compulsory voting and voter information seeking." *Research & Politics*, 5(1), 1–8.

Skalaban, A. (1988). "Do the polls affect elections? Some 1980 evidence." *Political Behavior*, 10(2), 136–150.

Slothuus, R. and de Vreese, C.H. (2010). "Political parties, motivated reasoning, and issue framing effects." *Journal of Politics*, 72(3), 630–645.

Smets, K. and Van Ham, C. (2013). "The embarrassment of riches? A meta-analysis of individual-level research on voter turnout." *Electoral Studies*, 32(2), 344–359.

Sniderman, P.M., Brody, R.A., and Tetlock, P.E. (1991). *Reasoning and choice: Explorations in political psychology.* Cambridge: Cambridge University Press.

Soroka, S. and Andrew, B. (2010). "Media coverage of Canadian elections: Horse-race coverage and negativity in election campaigns." in Sampert, S., & Trimble, L.J. (eds.), *Mediating Canadian Politics*, Toronto: Pearson Prentice Hall, 113–128.

Soroka, S., Loewen, P., Fournier, P., and Rubenson, D. (2016). "The impact of news photos on support for military action." *Political Communication*, 33(4), 563–582.

Splendore, S., Di Salvo, P., Eberwein, T., Groenhart, H., Kus, M., and Porlezza, C. (2016). "Educational strategies in data journalism: A comparative study of six European countries." *Journalism*, 17(1), 138–152.

Stolwijk, S.B., Schuck, A.R.T., and de Vreese. C.H. (2017). "How anxiety and enthusiasm help explain the bandwagon effect." *International Journal of Public Opinion Research*, 29(4), 554–574.

Sturgis, P., Nick, B., Mario, C., Stephen, F., Jane, G., Jennings, W., Jouni, K., Ben, L., and Patten, S. (2016). *Report of the inquiry into the 2015 British general election opinion polls*. London: Market Research Society and British Polling Council.

Sudman, S. (1986). "Do exit polls influence voting behavior?." *Public Opinion Quarterly*, 50(3), 331–339.

Tilley, J., Garry, J. and Bold, T. (2008). "Perceptions and reality: Economic voting at the 2004 European parliament elections." *European Journal of Political Research*, 47(5), 665–686.

Tilley, J. and Hobolt, S.B. (2011). "Is the government to blame? An experimental test of how partisanship shapes perceptions of performance and responsibility." *Journal of Politics*, 73(2), 316–330.

Tomz, M. and Van Houweling, R.P. (2008). "Candidate positioning and voter choice." *American Political Science Review*, 102(3), 303–318.

Traugott, M.W. (2001). "Assessing poll performance in the 2000 campaign." *Public Opinion Quarterly*, 65(3), 389–419.

Traugott, M.W. (2005). "The accuracy of the national preelection polls in the 2004 presidential election." *Public Opinion Quarterly*, 69(5), 642–654.

Tuchman, S. and Coffin, T.E. (1971). "The influence of election night television broadcasts in a close election." *Public Opinion Quarterly*, 35(3), 315–326.

Utych, S.M. and Kam, C.D. (2014). "Viability, information seeking, and vote choice." *Journal of Politics*, 76(1), 152–166.

Valentino, N.A., Beckmann, M.N., and Buhr, T.A. (2001). "A spiral of cynicism for some: The contingent effects of campaign news frames on participation and confidence in government." *Political Communication*, 18(4), 347–367.

Vandello, J.A., Goldschmied, N.P., and Richards, D.A.R. (2007). "The appeal of the underdog." *Personality and Social Psychology Bulletin*, 33(12), 1603–1616.

van der Meer, T.W.G., Hakhverdian, A., and Aaldering, L. (2016). "Off the fence, onto the bandwagon? A large-scale survey experiment on effect of real-life poll outcomes on subsequent vote intentions." *International Journal of Public Opinion Research*, 28(1), 46–72.

West, D.M. (1991). "Polling effects in election campaigns." *Political Behavior*, 13(2), 151–163.

Wilson, R.J. (1981). "Media coverage of Canadian election campaigns: Horserace journalism and the meta-campaign." *Journal of Canadian Studies*, 15(4), 56–68.

Wolfinger, R. and Linquiti, P. (1981). "Tuning in and turning out." *Public Opinion*, 4(1), 56–60.

Wright, M.J., Farrar, D.P., and Russell, D.F. (2014). "Polling accuracy in a multiparty election." *International Journal of Public Opinion Research*, 26(1), 113–124.

Zaller, J.R. (1990). "Political awareness, elite opinion leadership, and the mass survey response." *Social Cognition*, 8(1), 125–53.

Zaller, J.R. (1992). *The nature and origins of mass opinion*. Cambridge: Cambridge University Press.

Acknowledgments

This work has benefited from a number of sources. First and foremost, we wish to thank the Canadian Social Sciences and Humanities Research Council (SSHRC) for its generous financial support. Without this funding, our research would not have been possible.

Blake Andrew contributed in the early stages of this project. Blake's influence was key to the development of subsequent studies and the theoretical pillars upon which this work rests.

Our research also improved due to input from a number of colleagues. We especially acknowledge conference discussants who offered welcome feedback on various aspects of the project. In many cases, changes in our experimental design stem from the useful reactions we received.

Over the course of this work, a number of student research assistants were invaluable; thank you Abigail Gorrell, Dev Iyer, Bianca Jamal, Kourtney Koebel, Cynthia Cristina Leal Garza, Kristin Mead, Gabrielle Péloquin-Skulski, Daniela Sanchez Diaz, Rachel Weiss, and Thomas Wood.

We also recognize our editors and anonymous reviewers. Their insightful comments and recommendations were most helpful in refining our manuscript.

Finally, we are grateful to our families for their support throughout this project. We dedicate this manuscript to them.

Elements in Campaigns and Elections

R. Michael Alvarez
California Institute of Technology
R. Michael Alvarez is Professor of Political and Computational Social Science at Caltech. His current research focuses on election administration and technology, campaigns and elections, and computational modeling.

Emily Beaulieu Bacchus
University of Kentucky
Emily Beaulieu Bacchus is Associate Professor of Political Science and Director of International Studies at the University of Kentucky. She is an expert in political institutions and contentious politics – focusing much of her work on perceptions of election fraud and electoral protests. *Electoral Protest and Democracy in the Developing World* was published with Cambridge University Press in 2014.

Charles Stewart III
Massachusetts Institute of Technology
Charles Stewart III is the Kenan Sahin Distinguished Professor of Political Science at MIT. His research and teaching focus on American politics, election administration, and legislative politics.

About the Series
Broadly focused, covering electoral campaigns & strategies, voting behavior, and electoral institutions, this Elements series offers the opportunity to publish work from new and emerging fields, especially those at the interface of technology, elections, and global electoral trends.

We seek authoritative manuscripts and cutting edge work on electoral institutions and the administration of elections; election and campaign technology; political campaign strategy, tactics, and communications; campaign finance and spending; polling, surveying, and predictive modeling for political campaigns; participation in politics and turnout; voting behavior; emotions, political, and cognitive psychology; and voter mobilization. While much of the work in this field is quantitative or formal/ game-theoretic in nature, we encourage submissions that use multiple methods, including qualitative methodologies and creative ways of integrating empirics. For quantitative research, we will seek to integrate data and code into published manuscripts; and for mixed or qualitative methods, we will work on creative ways of integrating empirical data such as images, interview texts or recordings, or archival documents.

Cambridge Elements ≡

Elements in Campaigns and Elections

Printed in the United States
by Baker & Taylor Publisher Services